D0089982

3ω
/9
22

RIUS, pseudonym of Eduardo del Rio, was born in Michoacán, Mexico, in 1934. His work has appeared in the principal newspapers and magazines of Mexico, where he was chosen Best Editorial Cartoonist in 1959. He later was awarded the Grand Prize of the International Salon of Caricature in Montreal. He is internationally known for his political comic books.

because we love life
we can fight to the death..!

CUBA
FOR BEGINNERS

*

AN
ILLUSTRATED
GUIDE
FOR
AMERICANS
(and their
Government)
TO
SOCIALIST
CUBA

****

PATHFINDER

New York   London   Montreal   Sydney

ISBN 0-87348-128-3
Library of Congress Catalog Card Number 70-108717
Manufactured in the United States of America

First edition, 1970
Second edition, 1971
Fifteenth printing, 2003

Translated by Robert Pearlman

Pathfinder

www.pathfinderpress.com
E-mail: pathfinderpress@compuserve.com

PATHFINDER DISTRIBUTORS AROUND THE WORLD:

Australia (and Southeast Asia and the Pacific):
   Pathfinder, Level 1, 3/281-287 Beamish St., Campsie, NSW 2194
   Postal address: P.O. Box 164, Campsie, NSW 2194
Canada:
   Pathfinder, 2761 Dundas St. West, Toronto, ON M6P 1Y4
Iceland:
   Pathfinder, Skolavordustig 6B, Reykjavík
   Postal address: P. Box 0233, IS 121 Reykjavík
New Zealand:
   Pathfinder, P.O. Box 3025, Auckland
Sweden:
   Pathfinder, Domargränd 16, S-129 47, Hägersten
United Kingdom (and Europe, Africa, Middle East, and South Asia):
   Pathfinder, 47 The Cut, London, SE1 8LF
United States (and Caribbean, Latin America, and East Asia):
   Pathfinder Books, 545 8th Avenue, 14th floor, New York, NY 10018

CARTOONS FROM MEXICAN, CUBAN,
CANADIAN AND AMERICAN COLLEAGUES
APPEAR (MOSTLY INVOLUNTARILY)
IN THIS BOOK. I WANT TO SAY
THANKS TO ALL OF THEM.

As
EVERYONE KNOWS,
CUBA HAS
ALWAYS BEEN IN
THE SAME PLACE.
  EVEN COLUMBUS
FOUND IT ON
OCTOBER 28, 1492
AND SAID:
"THIS IS THE MOST
BEAUTIFUL LAND
MY EYES HAVE SEEN.."
  WITH THAT SAID,
HE TOOK POSSESSION
OF THE ISLAND IN
THE NAME OF
QUEEN ISABEL AND
SET UP THE
CUSTOMHOUSE...

HI..!
I DECLARE
TODAY "DAY
OF THE RACE"!
(THE WHITE
RACE, OF
COURSE..)

15

COLUMBUS' CREW THOUGHT THEY HAD ARRIVED AT BOMBAY AND CALLED THE TAINOS, SIBONEYES AND GUANATABEYES WHO WERE THE OWNERS OF THE ISLAND "INDIANS".

THEY WERE PEACEFUL AND SMOKED LARGE CIGARS (THE TYPE THAT ONLY CHE GUEVARA WAS CAPABLE OF SMOKING) AND LIVED DEDICATED TO THE PRODUCTION OF CHILDREN, SINCE THE LAND PRODUCED EVERYTHING, WITHOUT THE AID OF THE UNITED FRUIT CO., THE ALLIANCE FOR PROGRESS OR THE FORD FOUNDATION...

THE FIRST PROBLEM THAT CAME UP WAS THAT OF NAMING THE ISLAND; SOMEBODY WHO WANTED TO GET AHEAD PROPOSED THAT IT BE NAMED "JUANA", AFTER THE ROYAL PRINCESS...

JUANA? AND HOW DO YOU MAKE A "JUANA LIBRE"?

✳ "CUBA LIBRE" -RUM AND COKE- IS CUBA'S FAVORITE DRINK..

(AND FOR A TIME IT WAS SO NAMED... BUT WITH SUCH A SMALL NAME JUANA ISLAND GOT LOST ON THE MAPS...)

I HAVE A BEAUTIFUL, BEAUTIFUL NAME..!

... A PRIEST SUGGESTED ANOTHER NAME: "FERDINAND", WHICH, ALTHOUGH IT WAS LONGER, CREATED ANOTHER PROBLEM: NOBODY WANTED TO BE CALLED A "FERDINANDAN"...

THEN ANOTHER PRIEST (THERE WERE A LOT OF PRIESTS) PROPOSED "SANTIAGO". BUT SOON NO MORE LETTERS ARRIVED: ANOTHER INGENIOUS PRIEST HAD ALREADY FOUNDED SANTIAGO OF CHILE..!

¿AND WHY NOT "CUBA"?

17

(..ONE OF THOSE WHO WANTS TO GET IN GOOD WITH THE PRIESTS PROPOSED THAT THEY NAME THE ISLAND "AVE MARIA"..)

AND SO IT WAS APPROVED... THUS IT SEEMS VERY ODD TO US THAT THE ISLAND IS NOW CALLED "CUBA"...

IT SEEMS LIKE THERE WAS SOME SABOTAGE BY THE NATIVES, WHO WERE ATHEISTS OF SORTS...

* * * * * * * * * * *
WHAT NOBODY KNOWS IS WHAT THE WORD "CUBA" MEANS. (AT LEAST, I DON'T... SORRY !)
* * * * * * * * * * *

THE INDIANS EXTERMINATED, THE MISSIONARIES TRIED TO CONVERT THE REST TO CHRISTIANITY... BUT THEY ADORED IDOLS WITH INDIAN FACES, INSTEAD OF IDOLS WITH SPANISH FACES...

LEAVEST THESE THINGS: IF THOU TELLEST ME WHERE THE GOLD IS, THOU WILLST GO TO HEAVEN...

AND SINCE NO ONE WANTED TO BE A CHRISTIAN, THEY CAPTURED THE INDIAN CHIEF -HATUEY- AND TRIED TO MAKE HIM A CHRISTIAN.
  BUT HATUEY ASKED:
-"WHERE DO THE SOULS OF THE SPANIARDS GO?"
-"TO HEAVEN", REPLIED A PRIEST.
-"THEN"-SAID HATUEY- "I PREFER TO GO TO HELL.."
(AND THEY BURNED HIM ALIVE...)

Hatuey

THAT WAS ANOTHER CHRISTIAN SYSTEM USED LATER BY THE YANKEES, SPECIALLY IN VIETNAM...

BUT WHEN THE SPANIARDS WERE LEFT WITHOUT INDIANS, THEY REALIZED THAT THEY HAD BLUNDERED: WHO WAS GOING TO WORK? WHO WAS GOING TO SEED THE LAND, TO BUILD THE TEMPLES AND MAKE THE HOUSES...? CERTAINLY NOT THE SPANIARDS: THEY WERE CONQUISTADORES!!

NOT ME..!

SO THEY INVENTED ANOTHER SOLUTION: (WHICH THE YANKEES ALSO COPIED LATER), THEY BROUGHT BLACKS FROM AFRICA, SINCE IN THOSE TIMES YOU COULD GET THEM CHEAP..!

SO CUBA WAS CONVERTED INTO A SPANISH COLONY WITH A SYSTEM OF SLAVERY (BUT VERY CHRISTIAN).

THE KING OF SPAIN NAMED THE GOVERNORS, THE FUNCTIONARIES AND KEPT THE ISLAND QUIET WITH AN ARMY OF MERCENARIES... HOW PRETTY!

* *

LATER THE SPANIARDS BUILT FORTS ALL OVER THE COUNTRY (EXACTLY LIKE THE YANKEES IN NORTH AMERICA : ALL COLONIALISTS ARE THE SAME..!)

SUN

Havana Bay.

SOON THOSE LIVING IN CUBA SAW
THAT SOMETHING WAS WRONG:
THE ISLAND WAS VERY RICH,
BUT ALL THE MONEY WENT
TO SPAIN : THE SUGAR, THE
TOBACCO, THE FRUIT...
EVERYTHING WENT TO THE
ROYAL TREASURIES OF THE
SPANISH KINGS...

..AND THE ROMAN POPE..

ABAJO LOS GALLEGOS DE ALLA, REDIEZ..*

AS A RESULT, IN 1819
THE SPANISH OF CUBA
REVOLTED AGAINST THE
SPANISH OF SPAIN...

UNFORTUNATELY, ALL
THOSE WHO REBELLED
WERE HUNG...

24 ✳ Down with the Spaniards..!

LET'S HAVE ANOTHER BRAWL!

INDEPENDENCIA

BY THAT TIME ALL LATIN-AMERICA WAS FREE FROM SPAIN, EXCEPT CUBA!

SO, MORE INSURRECTIONS FOLLOWED: IN 1826, IN 1828, IN 1830, IN 1848, IN 1851, IN 1855...UNTIL IT BECAME A CUSTOM OF THE CUBANS...

MY CORN HURTS: THERE MUST BE AN UPRISING TONIGHT!

TO MAKE THE STRUGGLE A LITTLE MORE DIFFICULT, THE CATHOLIC MAJESTIES ORDERED SOME VERY "CHRISTIAN" LAWS...

LET'S GET AFTER THOSE NEGROES!

NO CUBAN COULD
OCCUPY a PUBLIC POST..

NO CUBAN COULD
SET UP AN INDUSTRY
OR A BUSINESS...

MARRIAGES BETWEEN
BLACKS AND WHITES
WERE ANNULLED,
EXCEPT IF ONE OF
THE PARTIES WAS A NOBLEMAN

NO CUBAN HAD THE
RIGHT TO A LEGAL TRIAL
AGAINST A SPANIARD..

NO CUBAN COULD TAKE
LODGERS IN HIS HOUSE..

NO CUBAN COULD
TRAVEL WITHOUT
MILITARY PERMISSION...

OH,
WESTERN
CIVILIZATION,
BOY !

AND WHAT
HAPPENNED..?

THAT NO
CUBAN COULD
PERMIT THIS,
MAN..!!

NO CUBAN
CAN GO TO
HEAVEN WITHOUT
PERMISSION..

26

PROBABLY AS A RESULT
OF THAT, WITH THE YEAR

68

CAME A RICH MAN ENRAGED
BY THE SITUATION:

EVERYWHERE
IN THE
COUNTRY,
OTHER
CUBANS
FOLLOW HIM:
AGRAMONTE,
FIGUEREDO,
GUTIÉRREZ,
MÁXIMO
GÓMEZ AND
ANTONIO
MACEO....>
(NEGRO)

CARLOS MANUEL DE CÉSPEDES
WHO LIBERATED HIS SLAVES
AND HEADED IN YARA A BIG
REBELLION AGAINST SPAIN...
TIRED OF SO MUCH SLAVERY,
THOUSANDS OF NEGROES, MULATTOS,
AND CAFE-AU-LAITS' ROSE UP IN
STICKS, SINCE THEY DIDN'T HAVE
ARMS...

THIS TIME THE REBELLION SEEMS SERIOUS!

27

WELL, MORE OR LESS SERIOUS: YOU KNOW HOW THE CUBANS ARE; WITHOUT MUSIC THERE IS NOTHING! AFTER MAKING THE REBELLION, THEY MADE THE MUSIC OF THE REBELLION: "THE BAYAMESA"...

♪ AL COMBATE CORRED BAYAMESES, AÉ, AÉ ♪

(TO BE SURE, IT WAS WITH MOZART'S MUSIC. AFTER ALL, NO ONE IS PERFECT, SPECIALLY IN WARTIME..)

* *

THE REVOLT LASTED TEN YEARS AND WAS SNUFFED OUT AT GREAT COST: 85,000 SPANIARDS AND 50,000 REBELS WERE KILLED (CÉSPEDES TOO)

NOW HE IS A NATIONAL HERO (A KIND OF WASHINGTON..)

So ENDED THE YEAR 1878... A CRY FILLED EVERY MOUTH: (PART OF THE MOUTH, ANY WAY)

The REBELLION CRUSHED, SPAIN MADE SOME CONCESSIONS: SLAVERY WAS ABOLISHED AND SOME REFORMS WERE PROMISED...

(REFORMS THAT REMAINED, -AS ALWAYS- PROMISES..)

IN REALITY, EVERYTHING STAYED THE SAME IN CUBA: THE LITTLE ISLAND REMAINED A RICH SEAM OF GOLD FOR THE SPANIARDS... AND FOR THE CUBANS, ALSO A RICH SEAM OF GOLD, BUT IN DREAMS...

SINCE I HAVEN'T WON THE LOTTERY, THERE HAS TO BE A REVOLUTION..

AS FOR DREAMERS, ONE OF THE BEST WAS A LITTLE MAN -SMALL ON THE OUT-SIDE AND BIG INSIDE- WHO WROTE POETRY AND WAS CALLED:

JOSE MARTÍ

EXILED FROM CUBA FOR "HIS SUBVERSIVE IDEAS", MARTÍ TRAVELED OVER HALF THE WORLD WORKING, RAISING MONEY, ORGANIZING CUBANS-IN-EXILE, BREAKING FEMININE HEARTS AND WRITING (IN PROSE) IN FAVOR OF... CUBAN INDEPENDENCE...

FOR EVERY GUN THAT YOU GET HIM, HE GIVES YOU ONE KISS AND FOUR POEMS..

✳ ⓖ ✳ ⓔ ✳ ⓖ ✳ ⓔ ✳ ⓖ ✳ ⓔ ✳ ⓖ ✳ ⓔ

DOING IS THE BEST WAY OF SAYING..

31

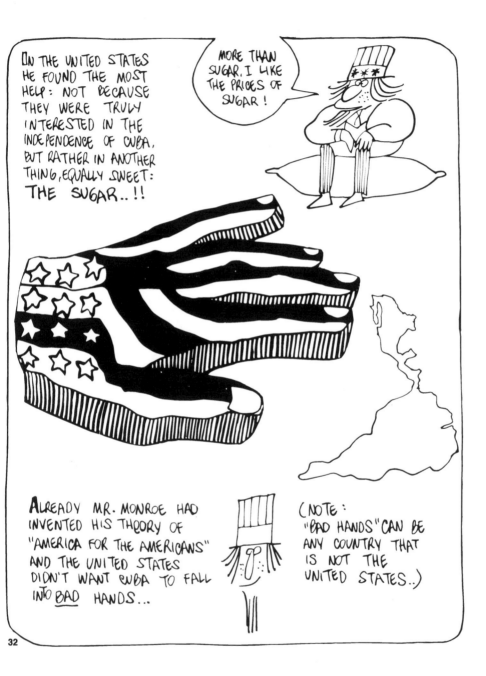

IN THE UNITED STATES HE FOUND THE MOST HELP: NOT BECAUSE THEY WERE TRULY INTERESTED IN THE INDEPENDENCE OF CUBA, BUT RATHER IN ANOTHER THING, EQUALLY SWEET: THE SUGAR..!!

MORE THAN SUGAR, I LIKE THE PRICES OF SUGAR!

ALREADY MR. MONROE HAD INVENTED HIS THEORY OF "AMERICA FOR THE AMERICANS" AND THE UNITED STATES DIDN'T WANT CUBA TO FALL INTO BAD HANDS...

(NOTE: "BAD HANDS" CAN BE ANY COUNTRY THAT IS NOT THE UNITED STATES..)

April 27, 1809 (Ibid, Vol. V, p. 444), Jefferson wrote as follows:

He (Napoleon) will with difficulty consent to our receiving Cuba into our Union, to prevent our aid to Mexico and other provinces. That would be a price, and I would immediately erect a column on the southernmost limit of Cuba, and inscribe on it a *ne plus ultra* as to us in that direction. We should then have only to include the North in our confederacy, which would be, of course, in the first war, and we should have such an empire for liberty as she has never surveyed since the creation; and I am persuaded no Constitution was ever so well calculated as ours for extensive empire and self-government. * * * It will be objected to our receiving Cuba, that no limit can then be drawn to our future acquisitions. Cuba can be defended by us without a Navy, and this develops the principle which ought to limit our views. Nothing should ever be accepted which would require a Navy to defend it.

I candidly confess that I have ever looked upon Cuba as the most interesting addition that can be made to our system of States, the possession of which (with Florida Point), would give us control over the Gulf of Mexico and the countries and isthmus bordering upon it, and would fill up the measure of our political well-being.

Henry Clay, while Secretary of State during the administration of John Quincy Adams, 1824-1829, writing to the United States Minister in Spain, said:

If the war should continue between Spain and the new Republics, and those islands (Cuba and Porto Rico) should become the theatre of it, their fortunes have such a connection with the prosperity of the United States that they could not be indifferent spectators.

President Buchanan in his annual message to Congress at the opening of the Thirty-sixth Congress, December 6, 1858, says:

Whilst the possession of the island would be of vast importance to the United States, its value to Spain is comparatively unimportant.

It is better then to lie still in readiness to receive that interesting incorporation when solicited by herself. For, certainly, her addition to our confederacy is exactly what is wanting to round out our power as a nation to the point of its utmost interest.

33

MARTÍ KNEW THIS AND CLEARLY SAW THE DANGER WHICH FACED CUBA: FREE HERSELF FROM ONE MASTER ONLY TO FALL INTO THE CLUTCHES OF ANOTHER, WORSE ONE...

" I LIVED IN THE MONSTER AND I KNOW ITS ENTRAILS.. EVERY DAY I AM IN DANGER OF GIVING MY LIFE FOR MY COUNTRY AND FOR MY DUTY TO PREVENT IN TIME, WITH THE INDEPENDENCE OF CUBA, THE EXPANSION OF THE UNITED STATES INTO THE ANTILLES AND OVER ALL OUR LANDS OF AMERICA..."

THINGS BEING WHAT THEY WERE, MARTÍ RENTED A BOAT IN KEY WEST AND GOT READY TO INVADE CUBA IN

95

SIMULTANEOUSLY OTHER RESTLESS PEOPLE INITIATED THE STRUGGLE ON THE ISLAND: THE OLD MACEO, PALMA, CROMBET, GÓMEZ AND SIX THOUSAND ANONYMOUS CUBANS WITH THE DESIRE TO BE INDEPENDENT...

WE'LL SEE WHO IS MORE STUBBORN: THE SPANIARDS OR US...

THE SPANIARDS DID NOT AGREE WITH CUBAN IDEAS; THEY ORGANIZED A LORDLY ARMY OF 95.000 MEN, SO THAT THERE WOULD BE NO DOUBT AS TO THE OUTCOME...AND STARTED THE SHOOTING AT THE HEIGHT OF THE CUBAN SPRING (MEANING, A DEMONIACAL HEAT..)

WHAT I'D DO FOR A COKE !

THE TROUBLE WITH THE START OF THE SHOOTING WAS THAT THE FIRST SHOT HIT JOSÉ MARTÍ ON MAY 19, 1895...!

WITH THE ORGANIZER AND SOUL OF THE MOVEMENT DEAD, THEY BELIEVED THE REBELLION WOULD QUICKLY PETER OUT. FORTUNATELY ONLY THE SPANIARDS HAD THAT IDEA...

MACEO, GÓMEZ AND MASSÓ DIDN'T SUSCRIBE TO THAT IDEA AND KEPT ON SMASHING THE SPANIARDS THROUGHOUT THAT YEAR.

BY 1896 THE CUBANS HAD A FORCE OF 60,000 MEN; THE SPANIARDS CALLED FOR REINFORCEMENTS, ENLARGING THEIR ARMY TO 200,000 MEN...

GOEST THOU AND HELP THOSE BEASTS TO GO QUICKLY TO HEAVEN...

LIKE LIGHTNING, HIGHNESS!

AND SUDDENLY A STRANGE ELEMENT APPEARED. AN AMERICAN BATTLESHIP DOCKED IN HAVANA "TO PROTECT AMERICANS LIVING IN CUBA": THE "MAINE"...

Meanwhile, in <u>CACARAJíCARA</u> THE CUBANS TOOK ADVANTAGE OF THE SPANIARDS' SLOWNESS IN LEARNING THAT NAME AND GAVE THEM A GOOD BEATING. IN MANZANILLO THE SAME. ALSO IN GUANTÁNAMO, AND ARROYO BLANCO AND GUAYAMO AND LAS GUÁSIMAS... SO THAT BY THE BEGINNING OF 1898 THE SPANIARDS DIDN'T WANT ANY MORE CHEESE, BUT RATHER WANTED TO LEAVE THE MOUSETRAP...

DESPERATE, SPAIN YIELDED AND CONCEDED TO CUBA HALF THE BARGAIN IN ORDER NOT TO LOSE ALL: AUTONOMY...

AND THAT'S WHERE THINGS WERE, WHEN SUDDENLY THE "MAINE" (WHICH WAS PROTECTING THE **50** MILLION DOLLARS OF AMERICAN INVESTMENTS) EXPLODED, KILLING THE ENTIRE YANKEE CREW... (FEBRUARY 15, 1898)

(AS EVERYBODY KNOWS, IT WAS AN UNFORTUNATE ACCIDENT...)

BUT THE UNITED STATES,
(ALWAYS PRACTICAL), BLAMED
SPAIN AND FOUND THE PRETEXT TO
INTERVENE IN CUBA. ON APRIL 21
PRESIDENT McKINLEY DECLARED WAR
AGAINST SPAIN "IN THE NAME OF GOD"...

I REMEMBER THE ~~ALAMO~~! MAINE !

IN THE UNITED
STATES NOBODY
WANTED THE WAR;
EVEN THEN THE U.S.
WAS BEGINNING TO
GET A BAD NAME.
BUT WAR IS
GOOD BUSINESS AND
THE PRESS (MISTER
HEARST) TOOK ON
THE JOB OF
INFLAMING "YANKEE
PATRIOTISM" BASED
ON FABRICATION
AND LIES ABOUT
SPAIN...

NATURALLY THE U.S. WON THE WAR (SPAIN WAS ALMOST DEFEATED BY THE CUBANS) AND IN PASSING TOOK POSSESSION OF PUERTO RICO, GUAM, THE PHILLIPINES AND A FEW OTHER LITTLE THINGS... IN EXCHANGE FOR THE "MAINE" AND 266 DEAD...   A BARGAIN!

AND THE UNITED STATES STILL HADN'T "INVENTED" THE COMMUNIST MENACE...!

IN REVENGE WE'LL SEND A FLAMENCO GROUP TO BROADWAY!

AND SO CUBA (THE CUBANS THOUGHT) ACHIEVED HER INDEPENDENCE (SIMPLE ONES..)

SPAIN LEFT CUBA : ON DECEMBER 10 THE TREATIES WERE SIGNED IN PARIS BETWEEN THE UNITED STATES AND SPAIN. AND CUBA ? WELL...

SOMETHING WAS SMELLING A BIT WRONG TO THE CUBANS...

So the Spaniards left Cuba...

RECONTRA COÑO!

LETS GET OUT OF HERE

#©*!!

A minute later, 15 infantry regiments, one of engineers and four artillery regiments arrived. The US Army began the "pacification" of Cuba...

FOR CUBA LIBRE!

The Spanish governor gone...

..enter Mr. Wood. Taxes were eliminated —to the king— and Cubans initiated payments to Washington...

41

THE SAME CAT BUT NOW, "ENGLISH SPOKEN", BLUE EYES AND "REPRESENTATIVE DEMOCRACY". THE GREAT FLAG OF THE STARS AND STRIPES WAVED OVER CUBA WITH THE INTENTION THAT IT WOULD FLY THERE "FOR EVER"... O-KEY!

HOWEVER, THE AMERICANS DIDN'T LIKE TO DO THINGS TOO AUDACIOUSLY; SO THEY INVENTED THE "PLATT AMENDMENT", TO TAKE OVER CUBA WITHOUT MAKING IT SEEM LIKE A FORMAL COLONY...

TRUE STORY OF THE PLATT AMENDMENT

The American Senate met to set the grounds for relations between Cuba and the U.S.

DO THEY KNOW HOW TO READ?

They rapidly wrote the "AMENDMENT"...aproved it... and presented it to Cuba FOR APPROVAL...

SURPRISE, MAN..!

And they gave Cuba one alternative: approve the amendment and the troops will leave... If not, they stay...

BUT... WHAT DEVILS DID THE PLATT AMENDMENT CONTAIN..?

THE SINFUL MEMORANDUM

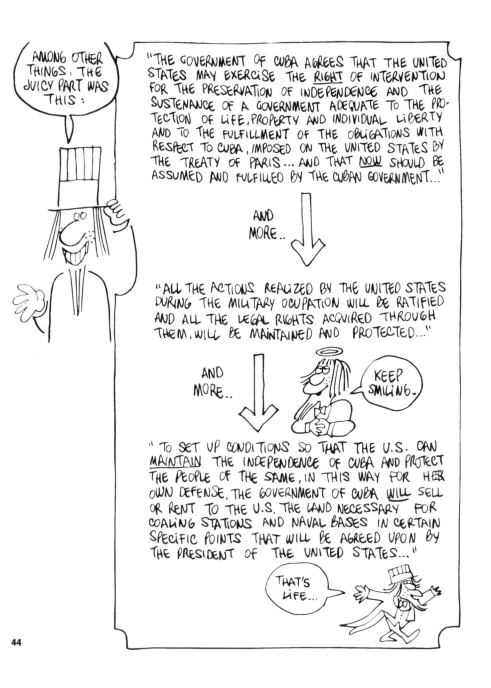

Not for love, but for force, "INDEPENDENT" Cuba began her new life under the gringo's knee... The United States had the key to mess around in someone else's house whenever it wanted to..!

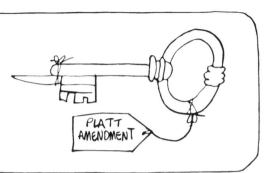

PLATT AMENDMENT

On the same ticket U.S. got a large territory: the Guantanamo Bay.. and they still have it (by the Platt Amendment, believe it or not..!)

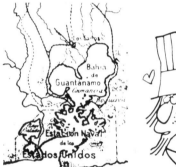

ONLY FOR SENTIMENTAL REASONS..

The logical president for Cuba was the hero and general **MAXIMO GOMEZ**, but.. he was radical and negro..!!!

So, United States put in one of its men: **TOMÁS ESTRADA PALMA**, who received orders directly from Washington... and his salary, also...

45

IN 1906 HE WAS REELECTED DESPITE POPULAR OPPOSITION... (BUT WITH U.S. PERMISSION). RESULT: ANOTHER REBELLION AND ANOTHER ARMED INTERVENTION OF THE U.S. "TO RESTORE ORDER"...

WE GOT TO GET USED TO DEMOCRACY...

AS A RESULT, THE U.S. QUIETLY KICKED OUT THE CUBAN GOVERNMENT AND NAMED AN AMERICAN—MR. MAGOON—PRESIDENT OF CUBA UNTIL 1909. MR. MAGOON TAUGHT THE CUBANS SOMETHING THEY HAD NOT KNOWN BEFORE: ADMINISTRATIVE CORRUPTION...

THE PORK BARREL, SIR!

(HE LEAVES CUBA A MILLIONAIRE..)

THE HANDING OUT OF POSTS, CONTRACTS, JOBS, GIFTS, FAVORS, ETC. WAS INTRODUCED BY THIS AMERICAN LAWYER TO THE ISLAND...

WELL: NOW IT'S A REAL DEMOCRACY..!

FROM 1909 TO 1913 GEN. J. MIGUEL GÓMEZ IS THE PRESIDENT:

AMERICAN INVESTMENTS: $400 MILLION..

FROM 1913 TO 1921 ANOTHER FRIEND OF AMERICAN INVESTORS: GEN. GARCÍA MENOCAL

THE AMERICAN INVESTMENTS REACH BY THAT TIME $1.200 MILLION DOLLARS..

AND FOR VARIETY, THERE WAS ANOTHER ARMED AMERICAN INTERVENTION FROM 1916 TO 1921. IT'S OBJECT? TO PUT DOWN STRIKES AGAINST THE SUGAR MILLS.. (AMERICAN-OWNED, OF COURSE)

BY 1925, THE U.S. CONTROLLED EVERYTHING IN CUBA : BANKS, MINES, TRAINS, SUGAR, CATTLE... AND THE GOVERNMENT. OH YES, AND THE TOBACCO.. !

VERY GOOD, INDEED !

47

IN THAT YEAR ANOTHER PRESIDENT WAS INAUGURATED: **GERARDO MACHADO,** MANAGER OF THE "AMERICAN AND FOREIGN POWER AND LIGHT COMPANY" AND THE FIRST CUBAN DICTATOR...

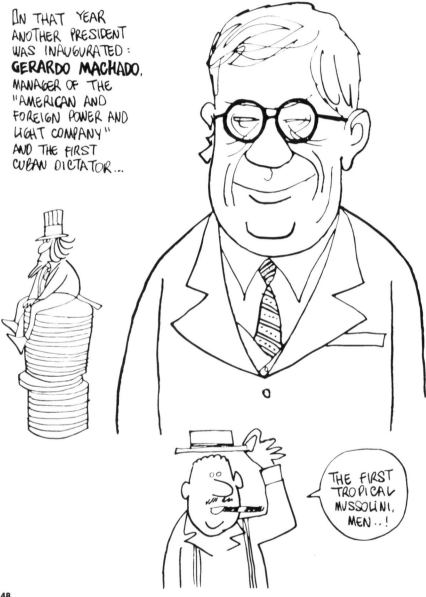

THE FIRST TROPICAL MUSSOLINI, MEN...!

MACHADO "GOVERNED" FROM 1925 TO 1933 (A RECORD!). HE HAD A "PERSONAL" POLICE FORCE OF 15,000 MEN. HIS POLITICS: TO MAKE HIMSELF RICH AND TO PROTECT AMERICAN INVESTMENTS. HIS METHOD: ASSASSINATE ANYONE WHO OPPOSED HIS GOVERNMENT, WHOEVER HE MIGHT BE...

(AS THOSE WHO OPPOSED HIM MOST WERE THE COMMUNISTS, MACHADO KILLED MANY OF THEM)

MANY STUDENT LEADERS WERE ASSASSINATED: JULIO ANTONIO MELLA, RAFAEL TREJO & OTHERS.
ANOTHER STUDENT LEADER, VILLENA, DIED IN JAIL..

BUT NOT EVERYONE THOUGHT BADLY OF MACHADO: MR. CALVIN COOLIDGE THOUGHT THAT "UNDER MACHADO CUBA IS A SOVEREIGN STATE...HER PEOPLE ARE FREE, INDEPENDENT, IN PEACE AND ENJOYING THE ADVANTAGES OF DEMOCRACY..."

WITH THAT OPINION, MACHADO COULD STAY IN POWER...

49

BUT YOU KNOW WHAT NON-CONFORMISTS THE COMMUNISTS ARE... IN 1933 THE COMMUNIST PARTY - AND THE STUDENTS- ORGANIZED A GENERAL STRIKE IN HIS HONOR, AND MACHADO HAD TO GO...

OF COURSE! → MIAMI

FOR THE FIRST TIME, THE POPULAR STRUGGLE IN CUBA HAD A NEW AND "STRANGE" BATTLE CRY:

DOWN WITH YANKEE IMPERIALISM!

YANQUIS GO HOME!

AND ALL BECAUSE - WHEN MACHADO FELL - THE UNITED STATES CONTROLLED **70%** OF CUBA...

THEY REALLY WENT WHOLE HOG!

After Machado, a provisional president was named: **Carlos M. de Céspedes**, a supporter of ending the "Platt Amendment"... Uncle Sam turned pale!

And this is where the sergeant enters..

Alarmed, Uncle Sam called on one of his dearest nephews: an obscure (both inside and out) sergeant, **Fulgencio Batista**, to put Cuba "in order"...

The sergeant got some other militarists together and had a "revolution". Thus on the 4th of September 1933, Céspedes fell, a "junta" took over for six days...and finally in came another president: **Grau**. Batista was promoted to colonel for his "campaign merits"...

GRAU WAS JUST LIKE THE OTHERS, BUT IN BACK OF GRAU THERE WAS A YOUNG MAN WITH RADICAL IDEAS:

ANTONIO GUITERAS.

THANKS TO HIS INFLUENCE, THE NEW GOVERNMENT ABOLISHED THE OLD "PLATT AMENDMENT", INTRODUCED NEW LAWS CONTROLLING FOREIGN PROFITS, PROMOTED UNIVERSITY AUTONOMY, THE RIGHT TO STRIKE...AND TRIED TO NATIONALIZE THE ELECTRIC (AN AMERICAN) COMPANY...

← NOTE: GUITERAS WAS NOT A COMMUNIST

RESULT?

UNCLE SAM CALLS BATISTA. GUITERAS IS ASSASSINATED, GRAU FALLS, WASHINGTON APPLAUDS, CARLOS HEVIA BECOMES PRESIDENT (FOR 3 DAYS ONLY) AND IS REPLACED BY THE GORILLA **MENDIETA**, BATISTA'S TWIN...

FROM 1935 TO 1940 COMES A COLLECTION OF BATISTA'S PRESIDENTS (WITH THE UNSELFISH HELP OF THE UNITED STATES): MIGUEL MARIANO GÓMEZ, LAREDO BRÚ...ALL WITH LESS VOTES IN THE ELECTIONS THAN OTHER "UNOFFICIAL" CANDIDATES...

* *

ELECTION YEAR...AND TO AVOID GOSSIP, IMPERTINENCE AND ALL THAT, BATISTA HIMSELF WINS (THIS TIME THE UNITED STATES AND BATISTA ABSTAINED FROM AIDING ANOTHER CANDIDATE..)

53

IT IS THE ERA OF ROOSEVELT IN U.S.A. AND CÁRDENAS IN MEXICO.. IT'S IN FASHION TO BE ON THE LEFT, -EVEN IN WASHINGTON- SO.. BATISTA CALLS IN THE COMMUNISTS TO COLLABORATE, PROMISES FREEDOM AND REFORMS... (SO AS TO BE ABLE TO WIN THE ELECTIONS WITHOUT FRAUD ..)

WITHOUT PAIN OR GLORY THE BATISTA REGIME PASSED : THE 2nd. WORLD WAR BROUGHT DOLLARS TO THE COFFERS AND STRONGBOXES OF THOSE ALREADY FILTHY RICH OWNERS OF SUGAR, TOBACCO, NICKEL, ETC. (AMERICAN FIRMS, ANYWAY...)

IN 1944 NEW ELECTIONS AND A "NEW" PRESIDENT: THE OLD **GRAU**, WHO -WITH HIS PREVIOUS EXPERIENCE- STOOD OUT AS THE MOST CORRUPT PRESIDENT... (CONSIDERING ALL PAST CHAMPIONS..)

PROSPERITY FOR THE CUBANS..! (AT LEAST, FOR MY FAMILY..)

DURING HIS REGIME, CUBA BECOMES THE USA'S BROTHEL..

MORE ELECTIONS IN 1948 AND ANOTHER PRESIDENT: **CARLOS PRIO SOCARRAS**, WHO SURPASSED ALL EARLIER RECORDS OF CORRUPTION, REPRESSION, PROSTITUTION, POLICE BRUTALITY AND ROBBERY...

(THE SAME WAS HAPPENING IN MEXICO, WITH PRESIDENT ALEMÁN..)

FOR THE WINNER AND NEW CHAMPION!

HOWEVER, SOMETHING GOOD CAME OUT OF ALL THE DIRT: A LOT OF DISGUSTED CUBANS FOUNDED THE **ORTODOX PARTY**, WITH EDUARDO CHIBÁS AS LEADER.

THEY RAPIDLY WON THOUSANDS OF SUPPORTERS FOR A RADICAL CHANGE IN CUBA.

THE ORTODOXES DIDN'T ASK FOR MUCH: HONOR, POLITICAL AND ECONOMICAL INDEPENDENCE AND SOCIAL JUSTICE; IN OTHER WORDS, LESS UNCLE SAM IN CUBA..

HMMMM, SOMETHING IS ROTTEN AROUND HERE..

55

THE ORTODOX PARTY BROUGHT ANOTHER SHOCK TO GOOD OLD UNCLE SAM: BY 1951, IT WAS ALREADY CONSIDERED A SURE WINNER FOR THE 52' ELECTIONS, HAVING THE ADDITIONAL SUPORT OF THE CUBAN COMMUNISTS..

BATISTA: I NEED YOU!

WELL... ANOTHER PARTY, THE "AUTHENTIC", PRESENTED BATISTA AS ITS CANDIDATE, BUT WITHOUT A BIT OF SUPPORT AMONG THE VOTERS...

VIVA LA DEMOCRACIA

★ MADE IN USA

BUT, WHO NEEDS VOTER SUPPORT WHEN YOU HAVE TANK SUPPORT..?

BATISTA DIDN'T HAVE THE LEAST CHANCE OF WINNING THE ELECTIONS...UNLESS THERE WERE NO ELECTIONS...

DO YOU KNOW WHO'S GOING TO WIN?

WELL, I KNOW WHO'S GOING TO LOSE..

PERHAPS BECAUSE OF THIS ON THE 10th OF MARCH 52, INSTEAD OF ELECTIONS THERE WAS A COUP DÉTAT

WITH THESE DEVELOPMENTS, THE DECENT * PEOPLE PROCLAIMED BATISTA THEIR SAVIOR AND EVEN CARDINAL ARTEAGA GAVE HIS BLESSING TO THE NEW REGIME...

DEMOCRACY SURVIVED IN CUBA..! AND TO PROVE IT, BATISTA ABOLISHED THE CONSTITUTION, DISSOLVED THE CONGRESS, OUTLAWED THE COMMUNIST PARTY, SURROUNDED HIMSELF WITH MILITARY BRASS AND ASKED UNCLE SAM FOR AID...

* THE DECENT PEOPLE ARE ASSUMED TO BE:

HIGH SOCIETY
THE BANKERS
THE LANDOWNERS
THE COLONELS
THE INDUSTRIALISTS
THE CLERGY
THE AMERICAN INVESTORS
THE LAWYERS
THE KNIGHTS (OF Columbus)
THE RACISTS,
ETC. ETC. ETC.

UNFORTUNATELY (FOR BATISTA) IN CUBA THERE WERE NOT MANY "DECENT" PEOPLE. THE MAJORITY WERE COMMON PEOPLE, A MASS OF "UNCULTURED" NEGROES, DYING OF HUNGER, "LAZY" AND "BACKWARDS", WHO DIDN'T UNDERSTAND THEIR "DEMOCRATIC" SOCIETY...

IN THE "FREE WORLD" DECENT COMES FROM "CENT"..

FREE SUN

A MASS WHO BEGAN TO PROTEST, DIRECTED BY THOSE "CRAZY ONES" THAT ARE ALWAYS AROUND. HALF QUIXOTES AND HALF REDS... LIKE **FIDEL**..

STUDENT LEADER, MEMBER OF THE ORTHODOX PARTY, FORMER STUDENT IN A JESUIT SCHOOL, REBEL AND "AGITATOR".. A "CRAZY" YOUNG **MAN** WHOM EVEN THE COMMIES COULD NOT CONTROL..

IDEAL

AND SO, WHILE THE COMMUNISTS WERE SAYING THAT THE CONDITIONS WEREN'T RIPE FOR AN ARMED UPRISING, FIDEL CASTRO RUZ GOT TOGETHER 150 "CRAZY" YOUTHS LIKE HIMSELF AND DECIDED TO START THE REVOLUTION AGAINST BATISTA'S TYRANNY.

THE WORST THEY CAN DO IS KILL US!

ON
JULY 26, 1953
FIDEL'S "CRAZIES" ATTACKED THE **MONCADA** GARRISON - IN SANTIAGO DE CUBA - WHERE THEY ENCOUNTERED OVER A THOUSAND PERFECTLY ARMED AND ENTRENCHED SOLDIERS..

etc →

BUT THE ATTACK FLOPPED, PARTLY OUT OF BAD LUCK (OF THE 150 MEN WHO TOOK PART IN THE ATTACK, ONLY 100 WERE IN COMBAT: THE REST GOT LOST IN THE STREETS AND THE SURPRISE ELEMENT FAILED...)

ONLY 30 SURVIVED, FIDEL AMONG THEM. THE REST WERE ASSASSINATED AFTER THE ATTACK, IN THE JAILS OR IN THE STREETS...

BATISTA WENT WILD AND ORDERED A SWIFT TRIAL FOR THE SURVIVORS...

THEY WERE SENTENCED TO 15 YEARS OF PRISON ON THE ISLE OF PINOS, EXCEPT FIDEL. WHO WAS GIVEN ONLY 19 YEARS OF FORCED LABOR, ISOLATED FROM THE OTHERS...

BAH: HISTORY WILL ABSOLVE ME..

(SUFFICIENT TIME FOR HIM TO GROW THE MUSTACHE, AND FOR THE GANG TO READ, STUDY AND ANALYZE THE MANY MISTAKES THEY HAD MADE; ABOVE ALL THEY SAW ONE THING: THEY HAD TO GET ORGANIZED AND DO THINGS IN A LITTLE LESS "CRAZY" WAY...

WE NEED TO LEARN WHAT ONE SHOULDN'T DO IN A REVOLUTION..

THEN WE OUGHT TO GO TO MEXICO, FIDEL..

MEANWHILE, BATISTA CONTINUES HIS WAYS AND BECOMES A GOOD TYRANT AMERICAN-STYLE...

THE STUDENTS, THE COMMIES AND THE WORKERS CONTINUED FIGHTING AGAINST BATISTA, WHO WAS NOW A FULL-BLOWN DICTATOR...

STRIKES, SABOTAGE, STUDENT DEMONSTRATIONS AND EVEN AN ASSAULT ON THE PRESIDENTIAL PALACE IN HAVANA MAKE BATISTA NERVOUS...

José Antonio Echeverría Catholic Student Leader assasinated by Batista

WHAT CAN I DO WITH THESE NUTS?

TO APPEASE THE PEOPLE, BATISTA "ORGANIZED" NEW ELECTIONS AND FREED FIDEL AND HIS GANG. IT WAS 1955...

THAT SAME YEAR THE "CRAZIES" WENT TO MEXICO. THERE WAS LITTLE TO DO IN CUBA, EXCEPT BE SHOT BY BATISTA'S POLICE...

WE'VE GOT TO GET BACK TO CUBA SOON; I CAN'T STAND THOSE "TACOS" *

RIGHT: THE SPICE IS KILLING MORE PEOPLE THAN BATISTA.

* TACO: MEXICAN HOT SPICE FOOD.

IN MEXICO THEY REORGANIZED THE GROUP, RAISED MONEY AND TRAINED CONSCIENTIOUSLY WITH GEN. BAYO, A SPANISH WAR VETERAN. THERE IN MEXICO AN ARGENTINIAN PHYSICIAN JOINED THE GROUP: **CHE** GUEVARA.

AND ON NOVEMBER 24, 1956, IN WHAT WAS PRACTICALLY A TOY BOAT, 82 "CRAZIES" SAILED FROM TUXPAN, VERACRUZ —WITH FIDEL LEADING— TO INVADE CUBA ...

THE PLAN WAS THIS:

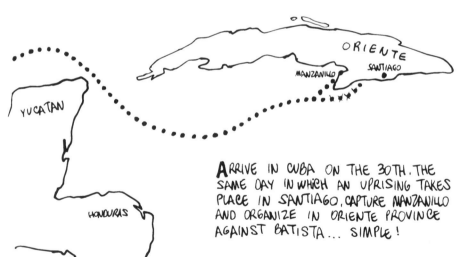

ARRIVE IN CUBA ON THE 30TH. THE SAME DAY IN WHICH AN UPRISING TAKES PLACE IN SANTIAGO, CAPTURE MANZANILLO AND ORGANIZE IN ORIENTE PROVINCE AGAINST BATISTA ... SIMPLE!

BUT A HURRICANE HIT THEM IN THE GULF OF MEXICO AND THEY ARRIVED ON THE COAST OF CUBA 2 DAYS LATE... ON A BEACH THAT WAS NOT THE RIGHT BEACH AND WITH A RECEPTION THEY WERE NOT EXPECTING: AIRPLANES OF BATISTA THAT BOMBED THEM..

THUS THEY LOST THE BOAT, THE WEAPONS, THE PROVISIONS AND 70 MEN: ONLY 12 SURVIVED. CUBA IS ALMOST FLAT, EXCEPT FOR ORIENTE WHICH IS LOADED WITH MOUNTAINS AND SMALL HILLS WHICH JOIN TOGETHER IN WHAT THE GEOGRAPHERS CALL "THE SIERRA MAESTRA"; IT HAS A PEAK, THE "TURQUINO", ABOUT 2000 METERS HIGH, AND ISOLATED FROM ALL CIVILIZATION...

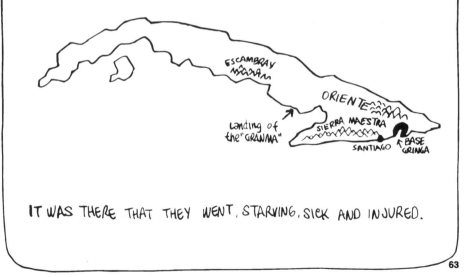

ESCAMBRAY

ORIENTE

Landing of the "GRANMA"

SIERRA MAESTRA

SANTIAGO

BASE GRINGA

IT WAS THERE THAT THEY WENT, STARVING, SICK AND INJURED.

BATISTA ANNOUNCED THE DEATH OF FIDEL AND DENIED THAT THERE WERE GUERRILLAS IN CUBA... BUT HERBERT MATTHEWS, REPORTER FOR THE "NEW YORK TIMES", CONTRADICTED HIM WITH PICTURES AND INTERVIEWS. THE WORLD KNEW THAT FIDEL AND HIS PEOPLE WERE ALIVE AND KICKING. BATISTA STOPPED LAUGHING...

THE TWELVE RESTED, MADE FRIENDS WITH THE CAMPESINOS OF THE SIERRA AND BEGAN TO GROW BEARDS...

THE SAME MONTH OF THEIR ARRIVAL, THEY INAUGURATED THE SEASON OF GUERRILLAS: THEY CAME DOWN QUICKLY, ATTACKED QUICKLY AND RETURNED EVEN FASTER TO THE SIERRA...

SOON VOLUNTEERS AND AID STARTED COMING TO THE SIERRA: ONLY BATISTA'S TROOPS COULDN'T FIND THEM BECAUSE "NOBODY KNEW" WHERE FIDEL WAS...

territorio LIBRE DE CUBA

WELCOME FREE CUBAN TERRITORY

THE "CRAZIES" STARTED TO BE FEARED AND UNDERSTOOD. THE COMMUNISTS AND THE ORTHODOX SENT AID AND REINFORCEMENTS. ALSO THE STUDENTS AND EVEN THE "CATHOLIC ACTION" YOUTH...

UP THERE THERE WAS NO BOOTY: THEY ORGANIZED THE WORK. PLANTED, MADE A BAKERY, SET UP A SMALL HOSPITAL, A RADIO STATION...AND CONTINUED READING...

ONE YEAR LATER THE "BEARDS" CONTROLLED ORIENTE PROVINCE, DESPITE BATISTA'S 20,000 SOLDIERS AND THE GRINGO MILITARY AID TO HIS GOVERNMENT...

FOR THE FIRST TIME, SOMEONE WAS HELPING THE PEASANTS WITH THEIR PROBLEMS: THE "BEARDS" WERE GIVING THEM MEDICAL AID...

CUBA WAS DIVIDED: THE GOVERNMENT AGAINST FIDEL AND...THE PEOPLE WITH FIDEL...

66

SOMETHING INCREDIBLE HAPPENED:
RAPIDLY THE PEOPLE FORGOT THEIR
IDEOLOGICAL DIFFERENCES AND
UNITED AGAINST BATISTA.
  IN THE "JULY 26 MOVEMENT"
(NAMED IN MEMORY OF THE MONCADA
ATTACK) THERE WAS EVERYBODY:
ANARCHISTS, CATHOLICS, STUDENTS,
COMMUNISTS, BOYS, WOMEN AND
OLD PEOPLE...

WE ARE ALL ONE!

AND WHILE FIDEL FOUGHT IN THE
SIERRA, THEY ORGANIZED THE FIGHT
IN THE CITIES WITH TERRORISM
AND SABOTAGE...

THE URBAN GUERRILLA, MAN!

BATISTA
RESPONDED WITH
AN ORDER:
"NO
WOUNDED,
NO
PRISONERS!"

THE FIGHT IN THE CITIES COST
MORE LIVES THAN 3 YEARS OF GUER-
RILLA WARFARE IN THE SIERRA:
BATISTA'S POLICE KILLED ABOUT
20,000 CUBANS... ALMOST ALL
YOUNG CUBANS.

Frank Pais

Abel
Santamaria

67

IN 1958 THE REBELS OPENED TWO MORE FRONTS LED BY CHE GUEVARA AND FIDEL'S BROTHER, RAUL. THE WAR GROWS QUICKLY...

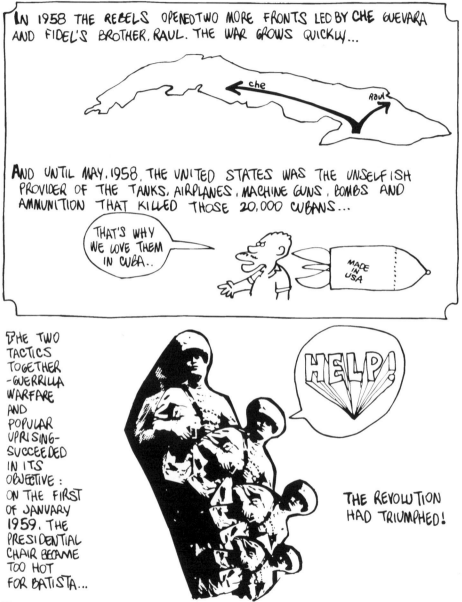

che
Raul

AND UNTIL MAY, 1958, THE UNITED STATES WAS THE UNSELFISH PROVIDER OF THE TANKS, AIRPLANES, MACHINE GUNS, BOMBS AND AMMUNITION THAT KILLED THOSE 20,000 CUBANS...

THAT'S WHY WE LOVE THEM IN CUBA..

MADE IN USA

THE TWO TACTICS TOGETHER -GUERRILLA WARFARE AND POPULAR UPRISING- SUCCEEDED IN ITS OBJECTIVE: ON THE FIRST OF JANUARY 1959, THE PRESIDENTIAL CHAIR BECAME TOO HOT FOR BATISTA...

HELP!

THE REVOLUTION HAD TRIUMPHED!

WHEN HE FLED, BATISTA TRIED TO "BEQUEATH POWER" TO SOME OF THE BATISTIANS WHO REMAINED...

ONLY THEY DIDN'T ACCOUNT FOR THE PEOPLE : A GENERAL STRIKE WITH THE SLOGAN: "ALL POWER TO THE BEARDS" MADE THEM CHANGE THEIR MINDS LIKE LIGHTNING...

THE MAGISTRATES NOMINATED TWO "NEUTRALS" (NO BATISTIANS, NO BEARDS): URRUTIA AS PRESIDENT AND MIRÓ CARDONA AS PRIME MINISTER...

VIVA CUBA, FRIENDS!

URRUTIA

MIRÓ

AND WHAT THE DEVIL DID THE UNITED STATES DO...?

VERY SIMPLE: ACCORDING TO THEIR NOBLE TRADITIONS THEY SENT **3** DESTROYERS AND **2** SUBMARINES TO HAVANA, TO SEE WHAT THEY COULD FISH...

WELL.. LET'S SAY.. TO SEE WHAT THEY COULD SAVE..!

IN ORDER TO
UNDERSTAND WHAT
HAPPENED IN CUBA
WITH THE TRIUMPH
OF THE REVOLUTION,
YOU HAVE TO TAKE
A GOOD LOOK AT WHAT
CUBA WAS IN

59

AT THE TRIUMPH OF THE REVOLUTION CUBA WAS— LIKE ANY OF THE COUNTRIES OF LATIN AMERICA— A "GREAT LITTLE DEMOCRACY"... PART OF THE "FREE WORLD" AND PRIDE OF "WESTERN CIVILIZATION"... A REPRESENTATIVE DEMOCRACY.

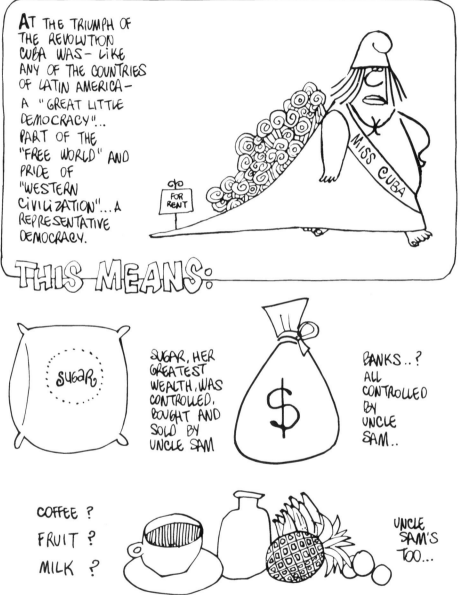

THIS MEANS:

SUGAR, HER GREATEST WEALTH, WAS CONTROLLED, BOUGHT AND SOLD BY UNCLE SAM

BANKS..? ALL CONTROLLED BY UNCLE SAM..

COFFEE ?
FRUIT ?
MILK ?

UNCLE SAM'S TOO...

AND WHO DO YOU THINK
SOLD EVERYTHING TO CUBA,
THAT IS :

MACHINERY, TOOLS, FOOD, COTTON, BEANS, WHEAT, CORN, FODDER, CARS, TRUCKS,
 CLOTHES, RADIO AND TV SETS, PAPER, TYPEWRITERS, ADDING
  MACHINES AND THE LIKE, RECORDS, PENS, TECHNICAL
   BOOKS, MEDICINE, SURGICAL INSTRUMENTS, CUTLERY,
    WHISKEY, GIN, LOCOMOTIVES, ELECTRICAL MATERIAL,
     SPORTING EQUIPMENT, CANS OF EVERYTHING
      IMAGINABLE, ELEVATORS, COCA-COLA, GUM
       LUMBER, GLASS, EVEN CIGARRETTES!,
        TOILET PAPER, OIL AND GREASE,
         LUBRICANTS, REFRIGERATORS,
          CHEMICAL INSTRUMENTS,
           THOROUGHBRED CATTLE,
            AIR CONDITIONERS,
             LOCKS, GANGSTERS,
              INDIA INK !!!
               SHOES, FISH,
                SOLDER,
                 PINS,
                 HATS..

I RECOMMEND
A SHOT OF RUM,
SO YOU CAN GET
THROUGH THE
FOLLOWING...

... ABRASIVES, SUITS, SOCKS, COLOGNE, EYE-BROW PENCILS, ENGINEERING AND DRAFTING EQUIPMENT, BRASSIERES AND PANTIES, FLASHLIGHTS AND CAMERAS, RAZOR BLADES, HOSE, SCISSORS. AIRPLANES OF ALL SIZES, HEATERS, CONTRACEPTIVES (A BASIC NECESSITY), STEEL PLATES AND BEAMS, YACHTS, NUTS AND BOLTS, SPECTACLES, SUNGLASSES, TOWELS, TOURISTS, BLENDERS, LENSES, MASCARA, BUTTER AND LARD, DOGS, TRUMPETS, TOILETS, SPRINKLERS, OXYGEN, CANDY, GAS, NYLON STOCKINGS, FILMS AND NEWSREELS, FISHING NETS, SHOE POLISH, LAMPS, HELMETS, FISH HOOKS, ALL TYPES AND KINDS OF MOTORS, LOTIONS, TOOTH PASTE, TOOTH PICKS, BARBER EQUIPMENT, CANNONS, JUKE BOXES, SOAP AND SOUPS, RIFLES, BICYCLES, BANKNOTES, SINKS, PISTOLS, SUITCASES, TANKS, FLOWER POTS, COINS AND PAPER MONEY, SHIRTS, SLEEPING PILLS, UNDERSHIRTS, LIQUOR, YEAST, RAILROAD CARS, DENTURES, CHAIRS, PAINTS, DRY CLEANING EQUIPMENT, RADIO AND TELEVISION STATIONS, PLUMBING EQUIPMENT AND ... WHEE!

DEPENDING (BODY AND SOUL) ON UNCLE SAM, THE REST IS EASILY EXPLAINED, AS IN ANY REPRESENTATIVE DEMOCRACY:

GOVERNMENT WAS CORRUPT, THE PRESS WAS CORRUPTED, POLITICIANS CORRUPTED THE TRADE UNIONS, BUSINESSES BECAME THE BASE OF CORRUPTION, THE ELECTIONS WERE ALREADY CORRUPT, HAVANA WAS THE MOST CORRUPT BROTHEL OF THE WORLD AND THE CORRUPT POLICE SERVED TO ASSURE THAT CORRUPTION DIDN'T END...

SOMETHING SMELLS AROUND HERE, BOY..

"SOMETHING" WENT WRONG IN CUBA, BUT THIS AND OTHER THINGS ARE COMMON IN ALL LATIN AMERICA COUNTRIES, EVEN THOUGH NELSON COMES "TO ASSURE" CHANGES WITH EVERY NEW AMERICAN PRESIDENT...

OTHER DEMOCRATIC
VIRTUES WERE NOT
LACKING IN CUBA:

IN 1958 THERE
WERE HALF A
MILLION
UNEMPLOYED
(IN A POPULATION
OF SIX MILLION)

EACH YEAR HALF
A MILLION CHILDREN
WENT WITHOUT SCHOOL.

BESIDES WHICH,
TWO-THIRDS OF THE
CHILDREN HAD NO
PRIMARY SCHOOL
TO GO TO...

FIVE MILLION CUBANS
(OUT OF A POPULATION
OF SIX MILLION)
DIDN'T HAVE THEIR
OWN HOMES AND LIVED
IN "BOHIOS" (HUTS)
WITHOUT LIGHT, WATER
OR SEWERAGE...

IN THE COUNTRY, THE PEOPLE WERE NOT EVEN OWNERS OF THE LAND THEY WORKED. THEY HAD NO SCHOOLS, NOR HOSPITALS; 10 THOUSAND TEACHERS WERE NEEDED AND ILLITERACY REACHED **43%** (1958)

FACUNDO FINALLY GOT HIS LAND...

FACUNDO

SURROUNDED BY THE SEA, THE POOR CUBANS COULD NOT GO TO THE BEACH BECAUSE THEY WERE PRIVATE (ESPECIALLY IF THEY WERE NEGROES)

WE DON'T HAVE TO ENVY THE U.S. ...WE HAVE DISCRIMINATION TOO..

THERE WAS LITTLE WORK; IT WAS BADLY PAID AND ASIDE FROM FOUR MONTHS OUT OF THE YEAR, THERE WASN'T EVEN THAT. AFTER THE SUGAR HARVEST EVERYONE WENT HOME TO STARVE...

"ON VACATION", SAID THE LANDOWNERS..

"THAT" IS WHAT THE REVOLUTION FOUND IN CUBA...

AS YOU CAN SEE, THE REVOLUTION HAD TWO BURDENS: CORRUPTION **AND** ECONOMIC DEPENDENCE, WHICH TOGETHER FORMED A SINGLE PACKAGE :

USA

WHAT A PACKAGE !

THE FUTURE DEPENDED ON UNCLE'S UNDERSTANDING...

SOON UNCLE BEGAN TO GRUMBLE INAPPROPRIATELY: HE PROTESTED ABOUT THE EXECUTIONS (WITH TRIAL) OF BATISTA'S ASSASSINS. PERHAPS BECAUSE HE HADN'T DONE IT WHEN BATISTA KILLED 20,000 INNOCENT PEOPLE IN THE STREETS AND JAILS...

(AS OPPOSED TO 550 SHOT BY THE NEW GOVERNMENT...)

NOT ONLY DO THEY SHOOT THEM, BUT THEY EVEN YELL "REMEMBER HIROSHIMA AND NUREMBERG" AT ME..!

79

THE "POOR INNOCENT" PEOPLE THE U.S. TRIED TO DEFEND WERE ALL THOSE POLICEMEN, MILITARISTS AND GUN-TOTING KILLERS WHO FOR YEARS AND YEARS MADE A LIVING KILLING PEOPLE...

OTHERS FELL INTO THE HANDS OF THE CUBAN PEOPLE, WHO COULD ONLY SETTLE THEIR OWN ACCOUNTS AND GIVE THEM WHAT THEY DESERVED...

DON'T YOU ACCEPT BRIBES?

MANY FLED TO THE U.S. (WHERE ELSE?) AND WERE USED TO "TESTIFY" AGAINST "CASTRO'S DICTATORSHIP" IN THE NEXT FEW YEARS...

THEY ARE NOT CHRISTIANS!

THE REST WERE JUDGED FOR THEIR SO INNOCENT CRIMES AND SENTENCED TO JAIL OR TO STAND BEFORE THE WALL. THE US DID THE ONLY THING IT COULD DO:

COME OUT IN DEFENSE OF THE KILLERS THEY HAD PREVIOUSLY TRAINED, ARMED AND LOVED...

IN THE FIRST MONTH OF THE URRUTIA-MIRÓ GOVERNMENT, MIRÓ (THE PRIME MINISTER) RESIGNED ON HIS OWN INITIATIVE. IN HIS PLACE, URRUTIA NAMED FIDEL CASTRO...

I'M LEAVING YOU THE PACKAGE..

UNCLE SAM AND THE RICH PEOPLE WERE NOT TOO HAPPY WITH THE CHOICE OF FIDEL, BUT THEY RESIGNED THEMSELVES TO IT...

FIDEL WAS NOT A COMMUNIST, BUT A NATIONALIST SIMILAR TO FIGUERES, BETANCOURT, LLERAS CAMARGO, OR HAYA DE LA TORRE... SO THOUGHT UNCLE SAM...

THEY ARE EASY TO HANDLE..

81

WITH A CABINET FORMED BY OLD POLITICIANS, FIDEL DECREED THE CONFISCATION OF THE LANDS OF BATISTA AND HIS FRIENDS...

WHAT COMES FROM WATER, RETURNS TO WATER..

GOD WILL PUNISH YOU FOR MESSING WITH MY FRIENDS..

AND HE FOLLOWED WITH THE PRINCIPAL ACTION, THE WATERMARK OF ANY AUTHENTIC REVOLUTION:

the agrarian reform

LAND TO THE TILLER !

THE LATIFUNDIOS (LARGE LAND HOLDINGS) WERE ELIMINATED AND THE LAND WAS GIVEN TO ALL THOSE WITHOUT LAND..

THE "OWNERS" PROTESTED, EVEN THOUGH THEY WERE OFFERED PAYMENT FOR THE CONFISCATED LANDS WITH BONDS OF THE NEW GOVERNMENT EARNING 4½ % INTEREST ANNUALLY...(NOT SUCH BAD BUSINESS FOR THEM!)

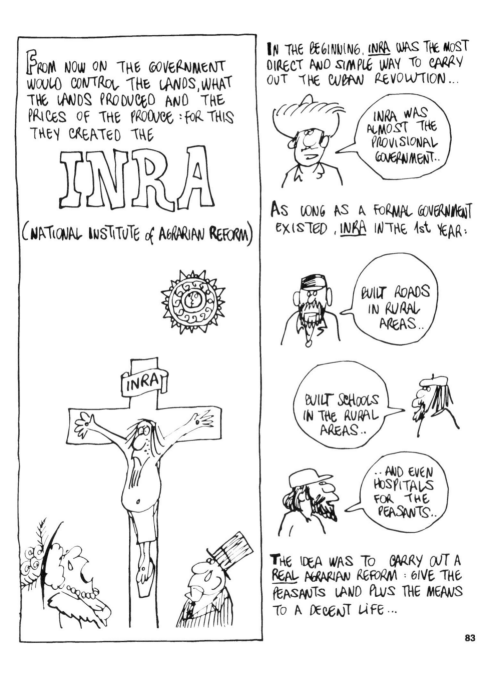

FROM NOW ON THE GOVERNMENT WOULD CONTROL THE LANDS, WHAT THE LANDS PRODUCED AND THE PRICES OF THE PRODUCE: FOR THIS THEY CREATED THE

INRA

(NATIONAL INSTITUTE of AGRARIAN REFORM)

INRA

IN THE BEGINNING, INRA WAS THE MOST DIRECT AND SIMPLE WAY TO CARRY OUT THE CUBAN REVOLUTION...

INRA WAS ALMOST THE PROVISIONAL GOVERNMENT..

AS LONG AS A FORMAL GOVERNMENT EXISTED, INRA IN THE 1st YEAR:

BUILT ROADS IN RURAL AREAS..

BUILT SCHOOLS IN THE RURAL AREAS..

..AND EVEN HOSPITALS FOR THE PEASANTS..

THE IDEA WAS TO CARRY OUT A REAL AGRARIAN REFORM: GIVE THE PEASANTS LAND PLUS THE MEANS TO A DECENT LIFE...

WELL, UNCLE SAM DIDN'T MUCH LIKE THE "AGRARIAN REFORM" EITHER... ESPECIALLY WHEN HE REALIZED THAT THE BEARDS WERE GOING TO DIVIDE UP THE AMERICAN-OWNED LANDS, TOO (75,000 ACRES)

NOR DID HE LIKE IT WHEN CASTRO CLOSED THE CASINOS, GIVEN THE COINCIDENCE THAT THE CASINOS WERE OWNED BY AMERICANS (GANGSTERS, TOO..)

YOU LOSE: IT CAME OUT RED!

AND HE WAS STUNNED WHEN HE LEARNED THAT FIDEL HAD LOWERED BY DECREE THE ELECTRICITY AND TELEPHONE RATES.. (BY PURE COINCIDENCE, BOTH COMPANIES WERE ALSO AMERICAN..)

WHAT A SHAME: THE REVOLUTION WAS GOING SO WELL..!

TWO MONTHS AFTER THE TRIUMPH, THE GOVERNMENT PROCLAIMED SOMETHING REALLY INCREDIBLE: THE **URBAN REFORM**

HOME, SWEET HOME..

FIRST, IT DECREED THAT PEOPLE PAY ONLY HALF OF THE RENT THAT THEY HAD BEEN PAYING...

(IMAGINE THE EXPRESSION ON THE FACES OF THE RICH APARTMENT BUILDING OWNERS..)

WHEN THEY SAID "REVOLUTION" I THOUGHT IT WOULD BE LIKE THE MEXICAN REVOLUTION!

BUT THIS WASN'T ALL: THERE WERE PEOPLE WHO HAD LOTS OF HOUSES BESIDES THE ONE THEY LIVED IN (HOUSES FOR VACATION, FOR RENT OR A "BACHELOR HOUSE", YOU KNOW..)

AS OPPOSED TO FIVE MILLION CUBANS WHO DIDN'T EVEN HAVE ONE..

85

THOSE "EXTRA" HOUSES FROM THE RICH PEOPLE WERE EXPROPIATED, TO GIVE THEM TO THOSE WHO DIDN'T HAVE ANY...

BUT NOT FREE: THEY WERE TO BE PAID FOR IN 5 TO 10 YEARS, AT THE VALUE DECLARED BY THE OWNER!

IF THE RICH DIDN'T WANT TO BE CHRISTIAN AND WILLINGLY GIVE UP WHAT THEY DIDN'T NEED, THE REVOLUTION WAS PREPARED TO TAKE IT... WILLINGLY..!

IT WAS ALSO DECREED (THE PEOPLE, ONCE IN POWER, HAVE THE RIGHT TO DECREE WHAT HAS NEVER BEEN DECREED BEFORE..) THAT EVERYONE WOULD BECOME THE OWNER OF THE HOUSE OR APARTMENT THAT THEY RENTED... AND THAT THEY WOULD KEEP ON PAYING THEIR OWN LANDLORD FOR THE FAMOUS PERIOD OF FIVE TO TEN YEARS...

THAT MIGHT BE CHRISTIAN, BUT VERY OLD ©*#!

THIS PARTIALLY RESOLVED THE HOUSING PROBLEM, THANKS TO THOSE FEW THOUSAND WHO HAD MORE THAN ONE.. (LIKE CASTRO'S OWN SISTER: JUANA; THE BACARDIS OR THE DUPONT FAMILY, ETC, ETC.)

IN HAVANA ALONE THERE WERE MORE THAN 300 BROTHELS, MORE THAN 700 BARS AND ABOUT... 15,000 PROSTITUTES..!

YANKI, COME HOME

AND THE BROTHELS?

AND THE BULK OF THE "CLIENTELE" CAME FROM THE UNITED STATES, WHICH CONSIDERED HAVANA "ITS" BROTHEL... (NOW IT'S PUERTO RICO)

MALE AND FEMALE, THE PROSTITUTES ARE NOW IN MIAMI OR MADRID. (ALONG WITH ALL THOSE WHO LIVED OFF PROSTITUTION AND EVERYTHING CONNECTED WITH IT..) ONLY 20 THOUSAND..

FIDEL ALSO LOWERED THE RATES FOR MEDICINES, TRANSPORTATION, HOTELS AND TOOK OTHER MEASURES FAVORING THE _POOR_...

HOW CAN YOU TRUST SUCH A GOVERNMENT?

ALSO HE DECREED THAT THERE WOULD NO LONGER BE PRIVATE BEACHS NOR COUNTRY CLUBS ONLY FOR RICH PEOPLE (NO PLAYBOY CLUBS IN CUBA...)
HE LOWERED THE PRICES OF CABARETS, THEATRE, MOVIES, BARS...AND BEGAN TO CONSTRUCT CHEAP HOUSES ALL AROUND THE ISLAND...

IT IS _IMPOSSIBLE_ FOR CUBANS TO SUPPORT THIS FIDEL..!

CONCERNING THE <u>PRESS</u> SOMETHING INCREDIBLE HAPPENED: WITH THE TRIUMPH OF THE REVOLUTION NOBODY TOUCHED THE NEWSPAPERS, NOR ISSUED ANY DECREES CONCERNING THEM...

DURING BATISTA'S REGIME, THERE WAS NO FREEDOM OF THE PRESS: HE ABOLISHED IT BY DECREE, ESTABLISHING CENSORSHIP BY THE GOVERNMENT..

> THE FOURTH ESTATE IS UNTOUCHABLE!

LIKE THE LATIN AMERICAN PRESS, THE CUBAN RECEIVED "SUBSIDIES", WERE REWARDED WITH OFFICIAL CONTRACTS AND PUBLISHED ONLY NEWS "MADE IN USA"... AND APPROVED BY THE GOVERNMENT

FIDEL'S NEW GOVERNMENT REESTABLISHED UNRESTRICTED FREEDOM OF THE PRESS... BUT TOOK AWAY THEIR SUBSIDIES...

AND THE CUBAN PRESS MAGNATES PROTESTED "SO MUCH" FREEDOM... AND BEGAN TO ATTACK THE "COMMUNIST" MEASURES OF THE NEW GOVERNMENT...

> MONEY TALK$!

> THIS FREEDOM MUST BE A COMMUNIST TRICK..!

89

THE PUBLIC, FOR ITS PART, REALIZED THAT THE PAPERS WEREN'T TELLING THE TRUTH AND SIMPLY STOPPED BUYING THEM...

AT THE SAME TIME, THE COMMUNISTS RESUMED THE PUBLICATION OF THEIR PAPER "HOY" (OUTLAWED BY BATISTA) AND THE 26th OF JULY MOVEMENT BEGAN TO PUBLISH "REVOLUTION" (NOW CALLED "GRANMA")

THUS, WITHOUT AN OFFICIAL SUBSIDY AND ALMOST WITHOUT ADS (THE AMERICAN ADVERTISERS HAD ALREADY STARTED TO LEAVE FOR MIAMI), AND WITHOUT SALES, SOME OF THE PAPERS BEGAN TO DECLARE THEMSELVES BANKRUPT...

WITH THE RADIO AND TELEVISION - FAITHFUL SERVANTS OF BATISTA - THE SAME THING HAD TO OCCUR : THEIR OWNERS WENT OFF TO THE "FREE WORLD" TO SELL TIME "ENGLISH SPOKEN"..

THERE IS NO FREEDOM IN CUBA.. AND NOW, A COMMERCIAL

THE PEOPLE OF THE ISLAND STARTED TO FLEE, FIRST THE KILLERS AND LATER THEIR ACCOMPLICES AND FRIENDS...

LIBERTY IS FINISHED!

THEN THOSE THAT EARNED THEIR LIVING FROM THE BROTHELS AND THE CASINOS AND FROM THE CLIENTS OF BOTH... AND THE POLITICAL HACKS AND THEIR ACCOMPLICES, AND THE BANDITS OF THE GOVERNMENT AND OTHER ENTITIES... AND ALL THOSE PEOPLE WHO HAD SOMETHING TO BE AFRAID OF...

OUTSIDE OF CUBA THEY ASKED WHY SO MANY PEOPLE WERE FLEEING... AND INSIDE CUBA THEY WERE THANKING GOD THAT SO MANY LOUSY PEOPLE WERE LEAVING...

CAN YOU IMAGINE: AFTER YEARS AND YEARS OF READING "LIFE EN ESPAÑOL", READER'S DIGEST... AND SEEING THE ANTI-COMMUNIST SLANDER IN THE MOVIES, ON THE TELEVISION AND IN NEW$PAPERS...

NOBODY KNEW WHAT COMMUNISM WAS, EXCEPT BY THE PROPAGANDA OF THE AMERICAN PRESS. IN TIME, MANY OF THOSE WHO FLEW TO MIAMI BECAUSE OF THE SLANDERS RETURNED TO CUBA (NOT EVERYBODY CHANGING THE "NATIONAL AIRLINES" ITINERARY, OF COURSE...)

SOME WHO DIDN'T GO TO MIAMI SCARED BY COMMUNISM DID SOMETHING WORSE: THEY TRIED TO FIGHT IT WITH WEAPONS... (DÍAZ LANZ, HUBERT MATOS, WILLIAM MORGAN) AND THEY CLIMBED THE SIERRA OF ESCAMBRAY ONCE AGAIN TO "COMBAT" COMMUNISM (WITH CIA HELP. NATURALLY..)

LONG LIVE COMMUNISM, DOWN WITH THE COMMUNISTS!

BUT THEY DIDN'T LAST UP THERE: THE PEOPLE THEMSELVES TOOK CHARGE OF BRINGING THEM DOWN AND CONVINCING THEM THAT THE REVOLUTION WOULD CONTINUE ONWARD, COMMUNIST OR NOT...

IF WHAT FIDEL DOES ARE COMMUNIST THINGS SIGN ME UP, BROTHER CAUSE THEY'RE MY "THING"... ♪

ANOTHER ONE CONFUSED BY THIS "COMMUNISM" WAS... PRESIDENT URRUTIA WHO HAD BEEN SIGNING THE "COMMUNIST" LAWS...

UNCLE SAM MIGHT GET ANGRY!

HE ASKED THAT "THE COMMUNISTS BE PURGED FROM THE REVOLUTION..". THE ISSUE WAS CLEAR: THEY WANTED TO DIVIDE THE PEOPLE WITH THE "PHANTOM" OF COMMUNISM..

IN THE SIERRA NO ONE ASKED WHO WERE REDS..

THUS, FIDEL SUBMITTED HIS RESIGNATION, CHARGING URRUTIA "OF ACCUSING THE REVOLUTIONARY GOVERNMENT OF COMMUNISM".. AND SO GIVING THE U.S. A PRETEXT FOR INTERVENING...

A LITTLE MORE TO THE LEFT, PLEASE...

IMMEDIATELY THE PEOPLE REACTED: FROM ALL OVER THE ISLAND PEOPLE CAME TO HAVANA TO ASK THAT URRUTIA RESIGN INSTEAD OF FIDEL...

¡FI-DEL FI-DEL FI-DEL FI-DEL !

WELL: URRUTIA RESIGNED AND FIDEL RETURNED.. AND IN URRUTIA'S PLACE, THE COUNCIL OF MINISTERS NOMINATED OSVALDO DORTICÓS, WHO CERTAINLY WASN'T A COMMUNIST EITHER...

...AND WHAT DID THE
HOLY MOTHER CHURCH DO...❓

THEY GAVE ME
A PRIZE IN THE
CARNIVAL
PARADE...!

* * * * * * * * * * * *

IN CONTRAST TO OTHER LATIN
AMERICAN COUNTRIES, THE
CHURCH IN CUBA WAS MORE
OR LESS A DECORATION...

CUBANS
SAY THAT
THEIR REAL
RELIGION IS
DRINKING
COFFEE...

(SO, THE
COFFEE-POT →
WOULD BE
THE
CATHEDRAL..)

Posada

97

FOR EVERY PRIEST THERE WERE **NINE THOUSAND** PARISHIONERS... AND SINCE IT WAS IMPOSSIBLE TO CARE FOR ALL OF THEM, THEY CHOSE TO DEDICATE THEMSELVES ONLY TO A FEW: THOSE WHO COULD PAY TO GO TO HEAVEN...

IT'S HARDER FOR A RICH MAN TO ENTER THE KINGDOM OF GOD THAN...

POLITICAL CHANGES NEVER AFFECTED HER: BATISTA CAME IN AND THE CHURCH WAS PRO-BATISTA... WITH MACHADO, MACHADIST AND WITH PRIO, PRO-PRIO...

YOU KEEP OUT OF MY BUSINESS AND I'LL KEEP OUT OF YOURS...

ON THE OTHER HAND, RELIGION WASN'T VERY IMPORTANT TO THE PEOPLE: ONLY **51 %** WERE (OFFICIALLY) CATHOLICS AND THE REST WERE INDIFFERENT, MASONS, AGNOSTICS OR SPIRITUALISTS...

AND TO FINISH QUICKLY: THE GREAT MAJORITY OF THE PRIESTS WERE SPANIARDS, AMERICANS OR ITALIANS...

WHEN FIDEL TRIUMPHED, THE CHURCH APPLAUDED THE NEW GOVERNMENT - AS WAS ITS CUSTOM - AND WAS READY TO ADAPT ITSELF — AS ALWAYS - TO THE NEW SITUATION...

THEY'RE "BEARDS", LIKE YOU..

EVERYTHING WAS FINE UNTIL FIDEL ANNOUNCED THE AGRARIAN REFORM AND THE NATIONALIZATION OF THE LANDS OF THE CHURCH (CONSIDERABLE)

REDS! LET'S CRUCIFY THEM, BY GOD!

AGRARIAN REFORM

(AFTER THAT, THE CHURCH BEGAN TO ATTACK THE "COMMUNIST" GOVERNMENT THROUGH SERMONS AND NEWSPAPERS ARTICLES...)

THUS, INSTEAD OF TAKING THE PEOPLE'S SIDE, THE CHURCH WENT ASTRAY, TOOK THE SIDE OF THE RICH AND BEGAN TO INTERFERE WITH FIDEL...

OUR FATHER, WHO ART IN MIAMI..

OR TO FOLLOW THEIR RICH PARISHIONERS TO MIAMI...

BY 1961 HALF OF THE PRIESTS WERE THERE. (ONLY THE TRULY CHRISTIAN REMAINED) AND THE PEOPLE DID THE OBVIOUS THING: THEY QUIT GOING TO CHURCH...

IN GENERAL, THE BEARD'S IDEA WAS TO CHANGE THIS STATE OF AFFAIRS AND MAKE CUBA AN INDEPENDENT COUNTRY, POLITICALLY AND ECONOMICALLY...

BUT UNCLE SAM HAD A DIFFERENT IDEA: HE WANTED EVERYTHING TO CONTINUE AS BEFORE...

WITH THE GOAL OF SETTLING THINGS AMICABLY, FIDEL WENT TO THE U.S. IN 1959, BUT THEY GAVE HIM THE COLD SHOULDER...

SORRY, I DON'T HAVE A LIGHT..

FIDEL'S BEARDS ASK FOR BONES, AND THEY GIVE 'EM STONES; THEY ASK FOR CRUMBS AND THEY GIVE 'EM NONE..

So THE BEARDS REALIZED THAT THEY WOULD HAVE TO CHANGE CUBA IN SPITE OF THE U.S. AND ITS INTERESTS...

SORRY : CUBA SÍ YANKEES NO !

NOT ONLY DID UNCLE SAM NOT WANT TO HELP THE NEW GOVERNMENT, BUT HE ALSO STARTED TO PLAY DIRTY TO CUBA...AND SO, IN JULY, 1959 BEGAN THE NEW PERIOD OF "FRIENDSHIP AND UNDERSTANDING", BETWEEN THE 2 COUNTRIES: AMERICAN PLANES NAPALM-BOMBED THE CUBAN CANE FIELDS...

US

WHAT A SHAME ! IT'S A CRIME !

UNCLE DENIED EVERYTHING. BUT SEVERAL DAYS LATER, ANOTHER YANKEE PLANE PILOTED BY AN EX-CASTROITE (PAID BY CIA) FLEW OVER HAVANA DROPPING LEAFLETS BLASTING FIDEL AND MACHINE GUN BULLETS (BOTH MADE IN USA).

101

CUBA HAD NO AIRPLANES AND TRIED TO BUY SOME (FOR DEFENSE AGAINST "OTHER" AIRPLANES) FROM ENGLAND...

THE LATE EISENHOWER (IKE) PROTESTED TO ENGLAND... AND ENGLAND NOTIFIED CUBA THAT "MAMA SAYS NO"

(IT WAS STILL 1959)

MORE? PROOF?

ON THE 18th AND 21st. OF JANUARY 1960 TWO MORE PLANES COMING FROM FLORIDA BOMBED THE SUBURBS OF HAVANA...

MORE?

ON THE 17th OF JANUARY EISENHOWER BEGAN (IN SECRET) THE TRAINING OF CUBAN REFUGEES TO ACT AGAINST CUBA "AT THE PROPER TIME"...

THIS WILL BE EASIER THAN THE NORMANDY INVASION..

STILL MORE?

AS THINGS WERE GETTING STICKY, CUBA TRIED TO BUY ARMS AND MUNITIONS IN THE USA...

AND SO UNCLE SAM, WHO HAD BEEN SELLING WEAPONS TO CUBA FOR 50 YEARS, NOW REFUSED TO SELL TO FIDEL..

AND STILL MORE:

IT WAS MADE CLEAR THAT "CUBA'S ATTEMPT TO OBTAIN THEM WOULD BE OPPOSED THROUGH EVERY POSSIBLE MEANS BY THE U.S.A.."

OH, FREE ENTERPRISE!

THAT IS WHY ON MARCH 4, 1960 THE FRENCH STEAMSHIP "LA COUBRE" MYSTERIOUSLY EXPLODED IN HAVANA DOCKS, KILLING 70 PEOPLE.. (THE **CIA** KNOWS THE EXACT NUMBER, OF COURSE)

(BY PURE "COINCIDENCE" THE BOAT WAS FULL OF ARMS AND AMMUNITION, WHICH CUBA HAD SUCCEEDED IN BUYING IN BELGIUM..)

Remember the Alamo, remember the Maine, remember LA COUBRE !

103

PRACTICALLY NOTHING: ONLY IT HAD MESSED WITH THE ECONOMIC INTERESTS OF THE UNITED STATES.. AND AS JOHN FOSTER DULLES SAID :

"THE UNITED STATES DOESN'T HAVE FRIENDS: IT ONLY HAS INTERESTS..."

WHAT ELSE HAD THE REVOLUTION DONE IN LESS THAN **ONE** YEAR THAT MADE THE USA ANGRY..?

IT HAD GIVEN HOUSES TO THOSE WHO DIDN'T HAVE ANY...
IT HAD GIVEN LAND TO THOSE WHO HAD NONE..
AND IT HAD GIVEN ARMS TO THESE PEOPLE, SO THAT THEY COULD DEFEND THEIR HOMES AND THEIR LAND...

WHAT OTHER LATIN-AMERICAN GOVERNMENT FOLLOWS OUR EXAMPLE ?

105

ANOTHER PROOF OF YANKEE FRIENDSHIP?

NOW COMES THE CASE OF THE PETROLEUM (THE OIL, YOU KNOW..)

CUBA DIDN'T PRODUCE ANY OIL (ONLY RUM). BUT THERE WERE REFINERIES WHICH PROCESSED AND REFINED THE CRUDE OIL BROUGHT FROM OTHER COUNTRIES...

HAVE YOU GUESSED WHO OWNED THE REFINERIES?

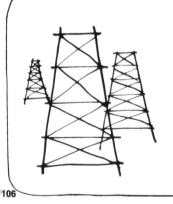

CUBA WAS OBLIGED TO BUY THIS OIL FROM THE YANKEE MONOPOLIES (ESSO, SINCLAIR, TEXACO) AND DELIVER IT TO THE YANKEE REFINERIES (ESSO, SINCLAIR, TEXACO), SO THEY COULD SELL TO CUBA — AT THE PRICES THEY SET- THE GASOLINE, OIL, ALCOHOL, KEROSENE AND ALL THOSE STRANGE THINGS WHICH ARE EXTRACTED FROM CRUDE OIL... AND SOLD WITH THE BRAND NAME ESSO, SINCLAIR, TEXACO..

BUT ONE DAY THE SOVIET MIKOYAN ARRIVED TO OFFER CUBA OIL IN EXCHANGE FOR SUGAR... AND FOR LESS MONEY THAN VENEZUELAN OIL (READ AMERICAN OIL, PLEASE..)

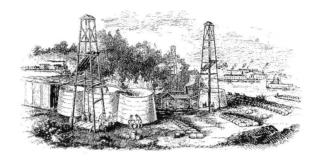

CUBA SIGNED THE CONTRACT..BUT THE GRINGO REFINERIES REFUSED TO REFINE THE SOVIET OIL, THUS HOPING TO BREAK THE BEARDED GOVERNMENT.

BUT:

LET'S SEE. ONE, TWO, THREE ... HEY, I'LL SAVE TWENTY MILLION DOLLARS A YEAR !!!

FIDEL, FIDEL YOU KNOW WHAT TO DO TO KEEP THE YANKS FROM MESSING WITH YOU.. ♫

..AND SINCE NOW IT WAS A MATTER OF EITHER PUT UP OR SHUT UP, CUBA NATIONALIZED THE YANKEE REFINERIES AND BEGAN TO REFINE THE SOVIET OIL..

MEXICO, CUBA, PERU..

107

UNCLE SAM FLEW INTO A RAGE AND WITHDREW ALL THE PETROLEUM TECHNICIANS... BUT THIS DIDN'T WORK EITHER: THE BEARDS TOOK CARE OF THE REFINERIES WITH MEXICAN (UNOFFICIAL) AID...

THEN UNCLE SAM HIT CUBA WHERE IT HURTS MOST:

THE AMERICAN GOVERNMENT (IKE) DECIDED TO BUY 1 MILLION LESS TONS FROM CUBA IN 1960.. AND TO BUY ABSOLUTELY NONE IN 1961

THIS WAS IN FACT A DECLARATION OF WAR: THE ONLY SOURCE OF INCOME CUBA HAD WAS SUGAR...

CUBA, HIT WITH A RIGHT CROSS, GOT UP AND REPLIED WITH A LEFT HOOK: IT NATIONALIZED ALL YANKEE PROPERTY!

(CUBA WAS READY TO FIGHT... IN SPITE OF THE UNEQUAL DISPUTE WITH U.S.)

BUT THE PROBLEM WAS STILL THERE: IF THE U.S. AND ALL ITS "ALLIES" REFUSED TO BUY ITS SUGAR, WHAT WOULD CUBA DO..?

SUGAR QUOTA

HEAR YE, HEAR YE, COME TO THE SLOW DEATH OF CUBAAA!

КОМИНТЕРН

* * * * * * * * * * *

ABANDONED BY ITS "FRIENDS", CUBA WAS SAVED BY NONE OTHER THAN THE "ENEMIES OF DEMOCRACY, LIBERTY AND GOD"...

THE USSR PROMISED TO BUY 700,000 TONS (AT A PRICE MUCH HIGHER THAN THE WORLD MARKET PRICE) AND CHINA WASN'T FAR BEHIND, ORDERING 500,000...

SUGAR

109

IT WAS THEN THAT UNCLE SAM STARTED SAYING THAT "CUBA WAS GOING COMMUNIST"... ALTHOUGH WITHOUT SAYING WHO WAS PUSHING HER THERE...

THE CUBAN REVOLUTION HAS BEEN BETRAYED!

COMMUNISM

SOON, ASIDE FROM THE PURCHASE OF SUGAR, THE USSR OFFERED SOMETHING MORE ON THE SAME TICKET: TO DEFEND CUBA AGAINST ALL AGGRESSORS...

CCCP

AFTER A YEAR OF BOMBINGS, SABOTAGE, ECONOMIC AGGRESSION AND OTHER ETCETERAS OF THE USA AGAINST CUBA, EISENHOWER APPEALED TO THE

OAS

"ORGANIZATION OF AMERICAN STATES", BUT YOU CAN CALL ME "COLONIAL DEPT. OF THE USA".

OAS

ACCUSING CUBA OF AGGRESSION..!!!

THE OAS CALLED A MEETING OF ALL LATIN-AMERICAN COUNTRIES IN SAN JOSE, COSTA RICA...

111

"Now for the evidence", said the King, "and then the sentence."

"No!" said the Queen, "first the sentence and then the evidence!"

"Nonsense!" cried Alice, so loudly that everybody jumped, "the idea of having the sentence first..!"

...AND SO THE **OAS** SENTENCED "AGGRESSIVE" CUBA AND REACHED THE "AGREEMENT" THAT CUBA WAS A "THREAT" TO THE ENTIRE HEMISPHERE.. (BELIEVE IT OR NOT, RIPLEY!!)

NOT SATISFIED WITH THIS, THE U.S. DECLARED ANOTHER HUMANITARIAN MEASURE AGAINST CUBA:

AN <u>EMBARGO</u> ON ALL GOODS GOING TO THE ISLAND FROM THE UNITED STATES...

CRACK
PRIZE BOXES,
SURE TO CONTAIN
SOMETHING OF INTEREST
FOR ALL.
With Directions for getting out of a Tight Place.

NOT EVEN A WHISKEY, BROTHER!

I DON'T KNOW WHY, BUT I'M BEGINNING TO SUSPECT THAT THEY'RE TRYING TO STARVE US TO DEATH...

..AND MORE: A CAMPAIGN OF SABOTAGE AND TERROR.   TERRORISTS PAID BY THE U.S. (CIA) BEGAN BURNING STORES, PUT BOMBS IN FACTORIES, MOVIES AND SCHOOLS... AND... ..ASSASSINATED PEOPLE INDISCRIMINATELY...

COMMUNISM IS INHUMAN! THE REDS ARE MURDERERS!

(MEANWHILE, EISENHOWER COMPLAINED THAT CUBA DID NOT "COOPERATE IN IMPROVING RELATIONS..."   GOOD!)

113

CUBA DECIDED, SINCE THE SITUATION WAS BECOMING SO BAD, THAT IT SHOULD ARM ALL THE PEOPLE.. LOOK-OUTS WERE POSTED, DAY AND NIGHT, HOUSE BY HOUSE, ALL OVER HAVANA...

THUS — IN EVERY BLOCK THE "COMMITTEES FOR THE DEFENSE OF THE REVOLUTION" WERE BORN... AND AS IF BY MAGIC THE WAVE OF TERROR AND SABOTAGE DECREASED...

MEANWHILE, AT THE UN CUBA DENOUNCED THE UNITED STATES FOR PREPARING AN INVASION OF ITS TERRITORY, TO BE LAUNCHED AFTER PRESIDENT KENNEDY TOOK OFFICE...

AN INVASION OF CUBA? THAT FIDEL IS CRAZY!

AS USUAL, THE HONORABLE **UN** SAT ON ITS HANDS WHILE THE UNITED STATES TRAINED ITS MERCENARIES IN GUATEMALA, HONDURAS, NICARAGUA (AND OF COURSE, IN FLORIDA, TOO!)

AND WHILE THE GRINGOS PLANNED TO INVADE CUBA AND DO AWAY WITH THE BEARDS, THE BEARDS ALSO INITIATED AN INTENSIVE TRAINING ALL OVER THE ISLAND, BUT A LITTLE DIFFERENT...

USA

CUBA

ON APRIL 10, 1961, 120 THOUSAND LITERACY WORKERS OF ALL AGES SPREAD OUT OVER THE ISLAND TO TEACH READING AND WRITING TO

ONE MILLION ILLITERATES

AND BY DECEMBER OF THE SAME YEAR, CUBA HAD LOWERED THE ILLITERACY RATE FROM 24% TO 3%, A FIGURE WE WOULD LIKE TO HAVE IN MEXICO (30% ILLITERACY)

WELL, I KNOW HOW TO READ... AND TO IDENTIFY AIRPLANES..!

WHILE THE CUBANS
WERE IN THAT CAMPAIGN,
ON APRIL 15, 1961
(FIVE DAYS LATER)
FLEETS OF AMERICAN
AIRPLANES PAINTED WITH
THE INSIGNIAS OF THE
CUBAN AIR FORCE,
LEFT FLORIDA AND
BOMBED THE AIRPORTS
IN HAVANA, CIENFUEGOS,
SAN ANTONIO DE LOS
BAÑOS AND SANTIAGO
DE CUBA, TRYING TO
WIPE OUT THE
REVOLUTIONARY AIR
FORCE...

AND THEY ALMOST DID, BABY!

WE DIDN'T HAVE MANY AND NOW WE HAVE EVEN LESS..!

AND IN THE EARLY MORNING OF THE 17th, 1500 MERCENARIES
INVADED THE ISLAND, WITH 5 AMERICAN SHIPS, 2 BATTLESHIPS,
AND 3 FREIGHTERS LOADED WITH TANKS AND ARTILLERY.. COMING
FROM NICARAGUA AND ESCORTED BY 2 DESTROYERS OF THE U.S.
NAVY...

LIBERTY

FOREVER!

C U B A

117

MR. KENNEDY'S PLAN WAS THIS: TAKE POWER IN A ZONE OF CUBAN TERRITORY... CREATE THERE A "PROVISIONAL GOVERNMENT"... WHICH WOULD IMMEDIATELY REQUEST HELP FROM THE UNITED STATES. WHICH WOULD (EFFICIENTLY) TAKE CARE OF THE REST...

ONLY MISTER JFK FORGOT ONE TRIVIAL DETAIL: THE CUBAN PEOPLE...

AS SOON AS YOU LAND IN CUBA, THE PEOPLE WILL RISE UP IN ARMS!

GOODY GOODY!

AND SO IT WAS: THE CUBAN PEOPLE ROSE UP IN ARMS... AND IN 48 HOURS DEFEATED THE INVADERS THAT CAME TO "LIBERATE THEM"..

BUT **LIFE** SAID THAT CUBA WAS A DICTATORSHIP!

THIS WONDERFUL CARTOON OF COLLEAGUE MacPHERSON SUMS IT ALL UP...

119

AND WHO WERE THESE "LIBERATORS".. ?

804.070 ACRES OF LAND
9.666 BUILDINGS AND HOUSES
70 INDUSTRIES
10 SUGAR MILLS
5 MINES
2 BANKS
2 NEWSPAPERS

WHICH THE REVOLUTION HAD TAKEN FROM THEM AND RETURNED TO THE CUBAN PEOPLE..

PLANTATION OWNERS,
WAR CRIMINALS,
EX-MILITARISTS,
LANDLORDS,
EX-POLICEMEN,
FUGITIVES,
PLAYBOYS
AND
BUMS ...

WHO INVADED CUBA DEFENDING THESE "PRINCIPLES":

THEY "ONLY" WANTED CUBA TO RETURN TO..

illiteracy
MISERY
PLANTATIONS

...AND TO ARISTOCRATIC CLUBS FOR THE RICH (NOW SCHOOLS FOR THE POOR), AND TO...

BEACHES "FOR WHITES ONLY.."

and to prostitution and schools only for the privileged and representative democracy...

THEY WANTED TO
RETURN THE RICHES
OF CUBA TO THE
GRINGOS.
RETURN TO
"FREE ENTERPRISE",
TO THE ROULETTE
WHEEL, TO
UNEMPLOYMENT, TO
THE "FOLKLORE" OF
SINGING CHA-CHÁS
WITH AN EMPTY
STOMACH...

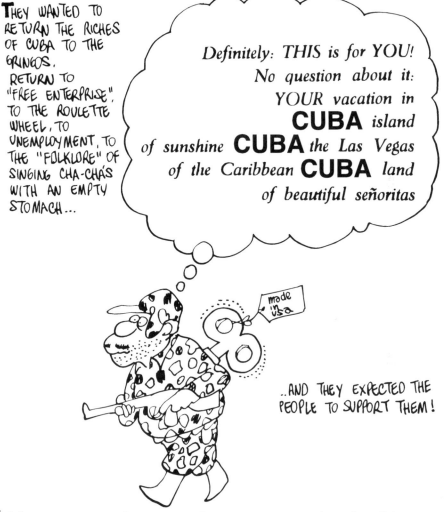

Definitely: THIS is for YOU!
No question about it:
YOUR vacation in
CUBA *island*
of sunshine **CUBA** *the Las Vegas*
of the Caribbean **CUBA** *land*
of beautiful señoritas

made in usa

..AND THEY EXPECTED THE
PEOPLE TO SUPPORT THEM!

(PARENTHETICALLY : THE THOUSAND AND SOME ODD TRAITORS WHO
WERE TAKEN PRISONERS - INCLUDING SOME PRIESTS - WERE GIVEN
BACK TO THEIR OWNER IN EXCHANGE FOR MEDICINES... FOR THE
FIRST TIME IN THEIR LIFE THEY SERVED FOR SOMETHING...)

THE INVASION HELPED CUBA MORE THAN A MARSHALL PLAN: IT DISPELLED ALL DOUBTS AMONG THE PEOPLE; EVERYONE JOINED THE REVOLUTION AND UNITED AGAINST THE COMMON ENEMY:

..AND NOW, AT LAST, FIDEL COULD SAY, ALTHOUGH IT HURT   UNCLE, THAT CUBA WAS GOING TO BE A

SOCIALIST REPUBLIC

CUBA COULD NOW EXPECT NOTHING (GOOD) FROM THE USA... BUT URGENTLY NEEDED TECHNICAL AID TO DEVELOP ITSELF... AND MILITARY AID TO DEFEND ITSELF.

WHO COULD GIVE THIS AID, AND IF POSSIBLE, WITHOUT STRINGS ATTACHED?

(GUESS →)

KENNEDY'S THREAT TO DO AWAY WITH SOCIALIST CUBA OBLIGED THE BEARDS TO ASK THE SOVIET UNION TO "LOAN" THEM SOME ROCKETS... THANKS TO THE OFFER MADE BY NIKITA KRUSCHEV.

BECAUSE OF IT AND THE "SOCIALISM", CUBA WAS EXPELLED (WITH USA AID) FROM THE OAS... AND IN OCTOBER 1962, KENNEDY TOOK ANOTHER STEP OF FRIENDSHIP TOWARDS CUBA: HE DECREED THE TOTAL AND ABSOLUTE BLOCKADE OF THE ISLAND...

THE PRETEXT FOR IT WAS "TO EXCLUDE THE ENTRY OF OFFENSIVE WAR MATERIAL"... HOW IS THAT..?

VERY SIMPLE: "OFFENSIVE" WEAPONS ARE THOSE OF THE ENEMY... AND "DEFENSIVE", THOSE OF THE UNITED STATES...

YOU CAN LAUGH AT THE OLD PIRATES: KENNEDY PUT THEM TO SHAME BY DECLARING THAT NO SHIP COULD GO TO CUBA WITHOUT HIS PERMISSION..!!

THINGS SOON GOT HOT: THE USA STATED THAT THEY WOULDN'T LET ANY SOVIET SHIP PASS WITHOUT "INSPECTING" IT... AND THE SOVIETS SAID THAT THEY WOULDN'T LET ANY GRINGOS INSPECT THEM...

AND SO BEGAN THE VERY FAMOUS CARIBBEAN CRISIS...

125

IN A FLASH THE
UN INTERVENED
(STRANGE THING)
AND GOT THE USA
AND USSR TO
TALK IT OVER
AND EVEN TRIED
TO INSPECT CUBA ..

THIS IS
NOT THE
CONGO,
MISTER .!

NIKITA TOOK HIS ROCKETS OUT OF CUBA (ANGERING THE CUBANS)
AND KENNEDY PROMISED NEVER TO INVADE CUBA, END THE BLOCKADE, etc

I PREFER THAT
TO THE THIRD-AND
FINAL- WAR ..

AND SO THE
MENACE WAS
STOPPED .. FOR
A WHILE : THE
BLOCKADE CONTINUES
AND THE IDEA
OF INVADING CUBA
IS STILL
FASHIONABLE
IN THE WHITE HOUSE
AND THE PENTAGON.

WE KNOW
NIXON ..

BESIDES FAILING TO DO WHAT IT PROMISED, THE UNITED STATES HAS CONTINUED TO HARASS CUBA WITH SPIES, SABOTEURS, PRESS CAMPAIGNS, AND WITH OTHER PROOFS OF DEMOCRATIC AND CHRISTIAN FRIENDSHIP...

WITH THE DANGER GONE (PHEW!),
CUBA FINALLY BEGAN—JUST IN
1963— TO BREATHE NORMALLY
AGAIN AND DEDICATE ITSELF
ENTHUSIASTICALLY TO THE
CONSTRUCTION OF

S O C i A L i S M

WHICH IS HARDER THAN MAKING THE REVOLUTION...

THE ONE IN CHARGE OF THIS KNOTTY
PROBLEM OF MAKING THE SOCIALIST
ECONOMY WAS ERNESTO GUEVARA,

ché

AN ARGENTINE DOCTOR, WHO KNEW AS
MUCH ABOUT ECONOMICS AS LYNDON
B. JOHNSON KNOWS RUSSIAN, BUT HAD
MANY IDEAS—NOT ALL OF THEM GOOD
FOR CUBA— AND ENTHUSIASM...

CHÉ WAS A DENTIST, YOU KNOW

THE PROBLEM WAS QUITE A PROBLEM: CUBA HAD NO TECHNICIANS, NO FOREIGN EXCHANGE, NO RAW MATERIALS, NO SKILLED WORKERS, NO ELECTRIC POWER TO SUPPLY THE NEW FACTORIES...

NOR MONEY TO GET ANY OF THESE THINGS SOON...

NOT EVEN A FACTORY TO MAKE MONEY...

IN SHORT, IT WAS A MATTER OF CONVERTING CUBA INTO A PRODUCER OF EVERYTHING IT HAD IMPORTED FROM THE USA:

THAT IS, EVERYTHING...

except one: SUGAR, THE ONLY CUBAN INDUSTRY.

129

TRYING TO PRODUCE WHAT THEY GOT BEFORE FROM THE US CUBANS MADE A BIG MISTAKE, REDUCING THE SUGAR AREAS AND SOWING THOSE AREAS WITH OTHER THINGS: TOMATO, RICE, VEGETABLES, ETC.

SUGAR, SUGAR SUGAR.. I AM TIRED OF THIS @*#! SUGAR!

※ ALL GOOD THINGS TO EAT, BUT NOT TO GET FOREIGN CURRENCIES, VITAL FOR GETTING RAW MATERIALS FOR THE CUBAN INDUSTRIALIZATION..

AS A RESULT SUGAR PRODUCTION LOWERED AND WE GOT PROBLEMS..

THEY HAD MANY PLANS AND IDEAS, ALL GOOD, BUT LACKED THE MAIN THING FOR A SOCIALIST ECONOMY: PLANNING...

ANOTHER THING WORKED
AGAINST CASTRO'S
EFFORT TO BUILD ITS
OWN ECONOMY: AS
AN EXAMPLE LET'S
CONSIDER THE CASE
OF A TIRE FACTORY...

A THE INSTALLATION : YANKEE

B THE CAPITAL : YANKEE

C THE MANAGEMENT : YANKEE

D THE ENGINEERS : YANKEES

E THE RAW MATERIAL : YANKEE

F THE SPARE PARTS : YANKEE

G THE FORMULAS : YANKEE

H THE KNOW-HOW : YANKEE

SO, WHEN THE TIME CAME TO NATIONALIZE THAT INDUSTRY (AND THE
OTHER AMERICAN INDUSTRIES) A LITTLE CHAOS APPEARED...

131

AND STILL MORE
PROBLEMS:

1

THE
AMERICAN
TECHNICIANS
LEFT...AND IN
THE PROCESS
TOOK ALONG THE
FEW CUBAN
TECHNICIANS...

2

THE FACTORIES
WERE WITHOUT
MONEY, FORMULAS
AND
MANAGEMENT..

3

THE UNITED STATES
QUIT SENDING RAW
MATERIALS AND
PROHIBITED OTHER
COUNTRIES FROM
SUPPLYING THEM
TO CUBA...

AND this
HAPPENED
TO aLL the
FACTORIES
THE YANKEES
HAD THERE...

DESPITE ALL THIS, NO FACTORY STOPPED IN CUBA, NONE ARE STOPPING NOW... (AND THE WAY THINGS ARE GOING, NONE WILL STOP)

THE CUBAN WORKERS TOOK THE PLACE OF THE GRINGO ENGINEERS... AND THE GRINGO ADMINISTRATORS.. AND THE GRINGO MILLIONAIRES.. AND THE FACTORIES KEPT RUNNING AS IF NOTHING HAD HAPPENED..!

THIS IS A JOB FOR UNDEVELOPED PANCHO !

THE FIRST YEARS OF REVOLUTION WERE HARD FOR CUBA

ECONOMIC ERRORS
LACK OF TECHNICIANS
DIFFERENT PARTS
LACK OF ECONOMISTS
BLOCKADE AND EMBARGO
LACK OF FOREIGN EXCHANGE
BAD ADMINISTRATORS
CIA SABOTAGE

RESULT: LESS TO EAT..

133

...AND WE LOST A LOT EXPERIMENTING...AND THE DROUGHTS AND HURRICANES WITH YANKEE NAMES...AND.. JUST LOOK AT THE MAP AND YOU'LL SEE ONE OF THE MAIN PROBLEMS WE HAD:

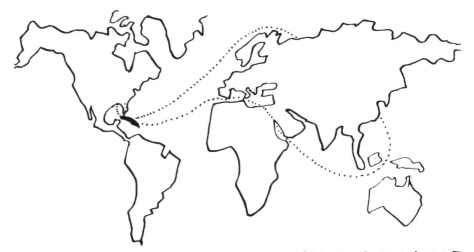

INSTEAD OF IMPORTING THINGS FROM MIAMI (90 MILES) WE HAD TO GET THEM FROM THE USSR OR CHINA OR POLAND (MORE THAN 10 THOUSAND MILES) AND NOTE THAT WE HAD NO SHIPS AT THAT TIME !!

.. THE CUBAN REVOLUTION THAT "WAS GOING TO DIE IN A YEAR", AS THE AMERICAN EXPERTS SAID, HAS DONE A LOT OF THINGS :

AGRARIAN REFORM
THE MOST COMPLETE IN ALL LATIN AMERICA ..!

(CUBA HAS DOUBLED ITS PRODUCTION SINCE 1959 AND IS DOING THE INCREDIBLE IN SUGAR: TEN MILLION TONS FOR 1970 !)

URBANreform

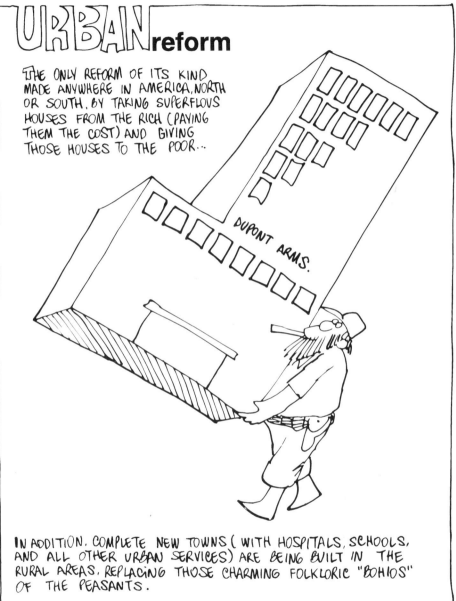

THE ONLY REFORM OF ITS KIND MADE ANYWHERE IN AMERICA, NORTH OR SOUTH, BY TAKING SUPERFLOUS HOUSES FROM THE RICH (PAYING THEM THE COST) AND GIVING THOSE HOUSES TO THE POOR...

DUPONT ARMS.

IN ADDITION, COMPLETE NEW TOWNS (WITH HOSPITALS, SCHOOLS, AND ALL OTHER URBAN SERVICES) ARE BEING BUILT IN THE RURAL AREAS, REPLACING THOSE CHARMING FOLKLORIC "BOHIOS" OF THE PEASANTS.

SPORTS

BEFORE, ALL SPORTS WERE PROFESSIONAL AND RUN BY AMERICAN GANGSTERS...

THE BEST BOXERS AND BASEBALL PLAYERS WERE SOLD IN THE INTERNATIONAL MARKET LIKE COWS..

TODAY, ALL KINDS OF SPORTS ARE PLAYED BY MILLIONS OF CUBANS. RESULT: IN THE 1968 OLYMPICS, CUBA WAS LATIN AMERICA'S BIGGEST MEDAL WINNER...

EVEN THE GOV'T MINISTERS PLAY BASEBALL. *

AND THE OLD PROFESSIONAL SPORTS (BOXING, BASKETBALL, FOOTBALL, BASEBALL, VOLLEYBALL, CYCLING) ARE ALL AMATEUR NOW...AND STILL MORE:

ALL SPORTING EVENTS ARE FREE !

* CUBA BEAT THE US. IN THE 1969 AMATEUR BASEBALL WORLD SERIES..!

ARMY & NAVY

THE REVOLUTION DISMANTLED THE GOVERNMENTAL (AND U.S. TRAINED) APPARATUS. IT DESTROYED THE ENTIRE PROFESSIONAL ARMY AND CREATED AN ARMY MADE UP OF THE REBELS THEMSELVES...

NUEZ

NO MILITARY REGIME, CUBA NEVERTHELESS HAS THE BEST ARMY IN LATIN AMERICA.. AND THE ONLY ONE WHICH WORKS FULLTIME IN THE RURAL AREAS BUILDING DAMS, HOUSES, SCHOOLS, ETC. AND WORKING IN NEW LANDS.. (AND THERE ARE NO GENERALS!)

139

POLITICS

THE CUBAN REVOLUTION SMASHED (AND SWEPT AWAY) THE OLD POLITICAL APPARATUS, GOT RID OF THE SENATORS, (INCLUDING SOME LOBBYISTS FROM THE US), GOVERNORS AND THE DEPUTIES AND CREATED A COLLECTIVE POWER OF THE PEOPLE... ELECTED BY THE PEOPLE IN FARMS, FACTORIES AND UNIVERSITIES...

SO..WHAT DO WE "NEED" ELECTIONS FOR..?

GOVERNMENT

THAT COLLECTIVE POWER IS THE CUBAN COMMUNIST PARTY, FORMED BY ALL KINDS OF PEOPLE (EXCEPT MILLIONAIRES) AND YOU KNOW THE PRIME MINISTER..

WE JUST CALL HIM "FIDEL" OR "THE HORSE"..

140

EDUCATION

I HATE STATISTICS AND I COULD JUST SAY THAT ALL EDUCATION IN CUBA IS FREE (EVEN COLLEGE), BUT IN 10 YEARS THE EDUCATIONAL GROWTH IS FANTASTIC...SO, PLEASE LOOK AT SOME NUMBERS:

	1958	1968
elementary schools	7,567 schools	14,753 schools
High School students	63,526	186,040
Normal School Students	1,279	6,800
Agrarian Schools	NONE	37
Fishing Schools	NONE	3
Scholarships	NONE	245,000
Teachers	21,806	68,583

BESIDES THAT, CUBA HAS SET UP SPECIAL SCHOOLS FOR EX-SERVANT GIRLS, FOR THE BLIND AND DEAF AND DUMB, FOR EX-PROS, AND TODAY IS SENDING HIGH SCHOOLS STUDENTS FOUR MONTHS A YEAR INTO RURAL AREAS...

TO LIVE WITH THE PEASANTS..

PLEASE MENTION AUDIOVISUAL EDUCATION!

ECONOMICS

THE BLOCKADE'S THE BEST THING THAT EVER HAPPENED TO THE REVOLUTION, BECAUSE THEY HAD TO INVENT EVERYTHING FROM THE BOTTOM UP, AND THAT'S GIVING THEM A SOUND ECONOMIC FOUNDATION...

TAKE THE FISHING INDUSTRY FOR EXAMPLE: CUBA IS SURROUNDED BY SEA, BUT THE PEOPLE NEVER EVEN ATE CHEAP FISH

WHY? WELL, FIRST CUBA HAD NO BOATS OR SHIPS.. AND ALL ITS FISHING WAS CONTROLLED BY AMERICAN COMPANIES..

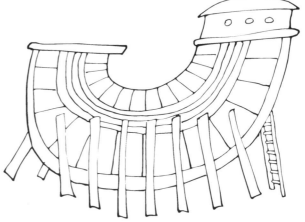

WAS..

NOW... SPAIN IS BUILDING SHRIMP-BOATS FOR CUBA, AND POLAND IS BUILDING MERCHANT SHIPS FOR CUBA, AND JAPAN AND BULGARIA, AND GDR (EAST GERMANY) ...AND CUBA NOW HAS ITS OWN SHIPYARDS... (SOUNDS GOOD, EH?..)

BUT NOW ALL THE SHIPS BELONG TO CUBA AND ALL THE FISH STAYS FOR POPULAR CONSUMPTION OR GOES FOR EXPORT...

IMAGINE THAT, MR. HEMINGWAY: CUBA EXPORTING FISH..!

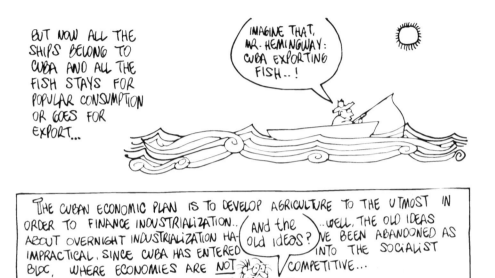

THE CUBAN ECONOMIC PLAN IS TO DEVELOP AGRICULTURE TO THE UTMOST IN ORDER TO FINANCE INDUSTRIALIZATION.. WELL, THE OLD IDEAS ABOUT OVERNIGHT INDUSTRIALIZATION HA- 'VE BEEN ABANDONED AS IMPRACTICAL, SINCE CUBA HAS ENTERED INTO THE SOCIALIST BLOC, WHERE ECONOMIES ARE NOT COMPETITIVE...

AND the old ideas?

THE SOCIALIST COUNTRIES DIVIDE AND DISTRIBUTE PRODUCTION SO AS NOT TO COMPETE WITH EACH OTHER MAKING CARS OR BUILDING FACTORIES. EACH COUNTRY "SPECIALIZES" IN CERTAIN ASPECTS. CUBA'S CONTRIBUTION IS TO DEVELOP HER AGRICULTURE AND CATTLE, ESPECIALLY TROPICAL CROPS LIKE SUGAR CANE & TOBACCO.

143

this doesn't mean that Cuba won't develop her industries!

NO?

BUT CUBA HAS NO PETROLEUM!

HER TENDENCY, HOWEVER, WILL BE TO CONCENTRATE ON LIGHT, COMPLEMENTARY INDUSTRY, SINCE RUSSIA, CZECHOSLOVAKIA AND EASTERN GERMANY HAVE ENOUGH HEAVY INDUSTRY TO PROVIDE ALL THAT IS NECESSARY, AND CUBA WOULD ONLY WASTE TIME AND MONEY TRYING TO COMPETE WITH THEM...

WELL... MAMA NATURE MADE CUBA A FERTILE ISLAND, WITHOUT POISONOUS CREATURES AND WITH AN ABUNDANT WATER SUPPLY...

and some mineral resources..

BUT EVERYONE THOUGHT SHE HAD FORGOTTEN TO SUPPLY CUBA WITH OIL, INDUSTRY'S BASIC ELEMENT. AT LEAST THAT IS WHAT THE AMERICAN EXPERTS ALWAYS SAID. HOWEVER, IT SEEMS THAT RUMANIAN EXPERTS (REMEMBER PLOESTI) HAVE LOCATED OIL!

IT'S CLEAR?

I'M ON CUBA'S SIDE, TOO...

MEDICINE

PRIVATE MEDICAL PRACTICE IS ALMOST NONEXISTENT IN CUBA NOW. CUBAN DOCTORS FEEL THAT PRIVATE PRACTICE IS UNETHICAL, ANTISOCIAL AND THAT IT TURNS THE PATIENT INTO A PIECE OF MERCHANDISE.

MORTAR BLUEPILL,
Graduate of the College of Pharmacy,
Practical Pharmaceutist.

PRESCRIPTIONS CAREFULLY COMPOUNDED.

CUBAN MEDICINE has been socialized

THERE HAVE BEEN PROBLEMS, OF COURSE. 2500 OF CUBA'S 7200 DOCTORS LEFT FOR FLORIDA AND IN ORDER TO PUT A SOCIALIZED MEDICAL PROGRAM INTO PRACTICE, CUBA NEEDED THOUSANDS OF NEW DOCTORS...

as well as appropriate facilities for free medical care!

HURRY UP!

THE REVOLUTION HAS BEEN ABLE TO COMPENSATE FOR THE ABSENT DOCTORS AND THE LACK OF HOSPITALS, AND DURING THE NEXT THREE YEARS 2500 NEW DOCTORS WILL BE ON HAND. BUT NOW, FOR THE FIRST TIME IN THEIR LIVES, MANY CUBANS IN THE RURAL AND MOUNTAIN REGIONS HAVE SEEN A DOCTOR AND RECEIVED MEDICAL ATTENTION...WITHOUT PAYING A CENT !

145

i puff!

LA HABANA - 1963

..and it is the only country in Latin America without ALCOHOLISM !

BOSSES NO LONGER EXPLOIT THE PEOPLE

AND THERE ARE NO MORE PIECARDS !

THE TELEPHONE IS FREE..

GIVE ME THE MOON..

AND THERE AREN'T ANY FAT, INSOLENT MILLIONAIRES...

DON'T LET JOHN PAUL GETTY FIND OUT!

EVERY ONE (WHO WORKS) HAS PAID VACATIONS..

SUN

THE MASS MEDIA BELONG TO THE WORKERS (AND NO MORE "READER'S DIGEST"!)

TIME-LIFE IS ANGRY WITH US!

147

CRIMES AND ROBBERIES ARE VANISHING

It sure is boring to be a cop..

RENTS AMOUNT TO ONLY 10% OF SALARY..

the landlords are in Florida, man!

THERE IS NO MORE UNEMPLOYMENT..

MIAMI. HERE I COME!

AND NO MORE DISCRIMINATION..

NO MORE VICE, GAMBLERS, ILLITERACY, MISERY, VAGRANTS AND SENATORS. PROSTITUTION AND DRUNKEN MARINES..

BAH: WE STILL HAVE PUERTO RICO!

IN SHORT: NO MORE "AMERICAN AID", NO MORE "FREE WORLD". NO MORE ROCKEFELLER'S VISITS, WORLD BANK AND CHARTER FLIGHTS..

NO MORE YANKEES!

BUT CUBA IS A DICTATORSHIP!

THE CUBAN "DICTATORSHIP" IS VERY PECULIAR: EVERYONE CALLS THE PRIME MINISTER BY HIS FIRST NAME AND CAN SEE HIM WHENEVER THEY WISH, MOST PROBABLY WHEN THEY RUN INTO HIM ON THE STREET...

STRIKE? YOU MUST BE CRAZY, FIDEL!

A DICTATORSHIP WHERE THE HIGHEST GOVERNMENT OFFICIALS PLAY BASEBALL IN THEIR SHIRT SLEEVES WITH THE REST OF THE PEOPLE..??

WHERE THE ENTIRE POPULATION IS ARMED AT ALL TIMES ????

A DICTATORSHIP WHERE EVERYONE KNOWS HOW TO READ?

A TOTALITARIAN DICTATORSHIP WHERE DECISIONS ARE MADE BY COMMON CONSENT

WHERE PROSTITUTES ARE SENT TO SCHOOL AND TAUGHT ANOTHER OCCUPATION..??

WHERE THE GOVERNMENT OFFICIALS MEET WITH THE WORKERS TO DISCUSS SALARIES AND PRODUCTION OR WHERE THE PEOPLE INTERRUPT THE PRIME MINISTER'S SPEECHES TO CRITICIZE CERTAIN MINISTERS OR OFFICIALS?

COME ON MISTER NIXON, MISTER ROCKEFELLER OR MISTER MILLIONAIRE: ASK THE AMERICAN PEOPLE TO COMPARE "DICTATORSHIPS" - THEIRS AND THE CUBANS'- AFTER INVESTIGATING THE FACTS, THAT IS..!!!

151

THE STATUS SEEKERS HAVE DIED OUT IN CUBA...

THEY HAVE NOW BEEN REPLACED BY MEN AND WOMEN WHO WORK VOLUNTARILY, WITHOUT CHARGING A PENNY, WITHOUT INTEREST IN MAKING MONEY OR STRIVING FOR A POSITION; MEN AND WOMEN WHO WORK TO THE POINT OF EXHAUSTION SO THAT THEY AND THEIR CHILDREN MIGHT SEE THEIR NEEDS FULFILLED...

AND TO PROVE THAT WE DON'T NEED AMERICAN "AID" TO BE HAPPY AND INDEPENDENT!

THE SO CALLED "IMPORTANCE" OF THE SECOND TELEVISION SET, THE LATEST MODEL CAR OR THE LATEST STYLE HAS BEEN REPLACED BY THE COLLECTIVE AND INDIVIDUAL SATISFACTION OF MEANINGFUL WORK (HARD, IT IS) BENEFITING EVERYONE..

NO COMPARISONS ARE GOOD: IT IS A DIFFERENT WORLD, BASED ON COMPLETELY DIFFERENT CONCEPTS THAN THOSE WE KNOW IN OUR SO-CALLED "FREE" SOCIETY FULL OF POVERTY AND INJUSTICE ...

CUBA - FORGET NUMBERS AND LIVING STANDARDS- IS CREATING THE POSSIBILITY OF A <u>NEW</u> MAN, OF A NEW SOCIETY BASED NOT ON MONEY BUT IN THE COMMON AND BETTER LIFE. CUBA IS A LIVING EXAMPLE OF A PEOPLE REALLY MOVING AND WORKING, A NATION SURVIVING AND GROWING AGAINST ALMOST IMPOSSIBLE ODDS.

MEXICO CITY / 1969

Also from Pathfinder

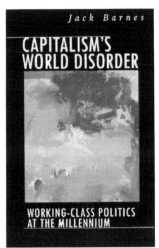

Capitalism's World Disorder

Working-Class Politics at the Millennium

JACK BARNES

The social devastation and financial panic, the coarsening of politics and politics of resentment, the cop brutality and acts of imperialist aggression accelerating around us—all are the product not of something gone wrong but of the lawful workings of capitalism. Yet the future can be changed by the united struggle and selfless action of workers and farmers conscious of their power to transform the world. $23.95

The Changing Face of U.S. Politics

Working-Class Politics and the Trade Unions

JACK BARNES

Building the kind of party the working class needs to prepare for coming class battles—battles through which they will revolutionize themselves, their unions, and all of society. It is a handbook for workers, farmers, and youth repelled by the social inequalities, economic instability, racism, women's oppression, cop violence, and wars endemic to capitalism . . . and who are determined to overturn that exploitative system and join in reconstructing the world on new, socialist foundations. $23.00

The Communist Manifesto

KARL MARX AND FREDERICK ENGELS

Founding document of the modern working-class movement, published in 1848. Explains why communism is derived not from preconceived principles but from facts and from proletarian movements springing from the actual class struggle. $3.95. Also available in Spanish.

Malcolm X Talks to Young People

"I for one will join in with anyone, I don't care what color you are, as long as you want to change this miserable condition that exists on this earth."—Malcolm X, December 1964. Includes his 1965 interview with the *Young Socialist* magazine. Now redesigned with an expanded section of photographs. In English and Spanish. $15.00

Socialism on Trial

JAMES P. CANNON

The basic ideas of socialism, explained in testimony during the trial of 18 leaders of the Minneapolis Teamsters union and the Socialist Workers Party framed up and imprisoned under the notorious Smith "Gag" Act during World War II. $15.95. Also available in Spanish.

Puerto Rico:
Independence Is a Necessity

RAFAEL CANCEL MIRANDA

In two interviews, Puerto Rican independence leader Cancel Miranda—one of five Puerto Rican Nationalists imprisoned by Washington for more than 25 years until 1979—speaks out on the brutal reality of U.S. colonial domination, the campaign to free Puerto Rican political prisoners, the example of Cuba's socialist revolution, and the resurgence of the independence movement today. $3.00. Also available in Spanish.

The History of the Russian Revolution

LEON TROTSKY

The social, economic, and political dynamics of the first socialist revolution as told by one of its central leaders. "The history of a revolution is for us first of all a history of the forcible entrance of the masses into the realm of rulership over their own destiny," Trotsky writes. Unabridged edition, 3 vols. in one. $35.95

Teamster Rebellion

FARRELL DOBBS

The 1934 strikes that built the industrial union movement in Minneapolis and helped pave the way for the CIO, recounted by a central leader of that battle. The first in a four-volume series on the class-struggle leadership of the strikes and organizing drives that transformed the Teamsters union in much of the Midwest into a fighting social movement and pointed the road toward independent labor political action. $16.95

Socialism: Utopian and Scientific

FREDERICK ENGELS

Modern socialism is not a doctrine, Engels explains, but a working-class movement growing out of the establishment of large-scale capitalist industry and its social consequences. $4.00

To See the Dawn

Baku, 1920—First Congress
of the Peoples of the East

How can peasants and workers in the colonial world achieve freedom from imperialist exploitation? By what means can working people overcome divisions incited by their national ruling classes and act together for their common class interests? These questions were addressed by 2,000 delegates to the 1920 Congress of the Peoples of the East. $19.95

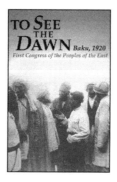

The Jewish Question

A Marxist Interpretation

ABRAM LEON

Traces the historical rationalizations of anti-Semitism to the fact that Jews—in the centuries preceding the domination of industrial capitalism—emerged as a "people-class" of merchants and moneylenders. Leon explains why the propertied rulers incite renewed Jew-hatred today. $17.95

Lenin's Final Fight

Speeches and Writings, 1922–23

V.I. LENIN

In the early 1920s Lenin waged a
political battle in the leadership of the
Communist Party of the USSR to
maintain the course that had enabled
the workers and peasants to overthrow
the tsarist empire, carry out the first
successful socialist revolution, and
begin building a world communist
movement. The issues posed in Lenin's
political fight remain at the heart of
world politics today. $19.95. Also
available in Spanish.

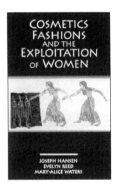

Cosmetics, Fashions, and the Exploitation of Women

JOSEPH HANSEN, EVELYN REED,
AND MARY-ALICE WATERS

How big business plays on women's second-
class status and social insecurities to market
cosmetics and rake in profits. The introduction
by Waters explains how the entry of millions of
women into the workforce during and after
World War II irreversibly changed U.S. society
and laid the basis for a renewed rise of struggles
for women's emancipation. $14.95

Thomas Sankara Speaks

The Burkina Faso Revolution, 1983–87

Peasants and workers in the West African country
of Burkina Faso established a popular
revolutionary government and began to combat
the hunger, illiteracy, and economic
backwardness imposed by imperialist
domination. Thomas Sankara, who led that
struggle, explains the example set for all of
Africa. $19.95

The Cuban Revolution

From the Escambray to the Congo

In the Whirlwind of the Cuban Revolution

Interview with Víctor Dreke

In this participant's account, Víctor Dreke describes how easy it became after the Cuban Revolution to "take down the rope" segregating blacks from whites at town dances, yet how enormous was the battle to transform social relations underlying all the "ropes" inherited from capitalism and Yankee domination. He recounts the determination, internationalism, and creative joy with which working people have defended their revolutionary course against U.S. imperialism—from Cuba's own Escambray mountains, to the Americas, Africa, and beyond. $17.00

Dynamics of the Cuban Revolution

A Marxist Appreciation

Joseph Hansen

How did the Cuban Revolution come about? Why does it represent, as Hansen puts it, an "unbearable challenge" to U.S. imperialism? What political obstacles has it overcome? Written as the revolution advanced from its earliest days. $22.95

Making History

Interviews with Four Generals of Cuba's Revolutionary Armed Forces

Through the stories of four Cuban generals—three of them leaders of the Cuban forces at Playa Girón that defeated the invaders in less than 72 hours—we can see the class dynamics that have shaped our entire epoch. We can understand how the people of Cuba, as they struggle to build a new society, have for more than forty years held Washington at bay. $15.95

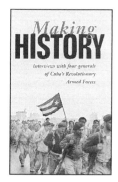

in today's world

To Speak the Truth
Why Washington's 'Cold War' against Cuba Doesn't End

Fidel Castro and Che Guevara

In historic speeches before the United Nations and UN bodies, Guevara and Castro address the workers of the world, explaining why the U.S. government so hates the example set by the socialist revolution in Cuba and why Washington's efforts to destroy it will fail. $16.95

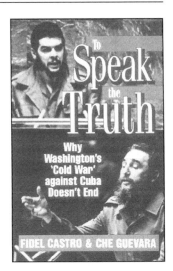

Che Guevara Talks to Young People

"If this revolution is Marxist, it is because it discovered by its own methods the road pointed out by Marx." Ernesto Che Guevara, 1960. Eight speeches from 1959 to 1964 by the legendary Argentine-born leader of the Cuban Revolution. Preface by Armando Hart, introduction by Mary-Alice Waters. $14.95

Episodes of the Cuban Revolutionary War, 1956–58
Ernesto Che Guevara

A firsthand account of the military campaigns and political events that culminated in the January 1959 popular insurrection that overthrew the Batista dictatorship. With clarity and humor, Guevara describes his own political education. He explains how the struggle transformed the men and women of the Rebel Army and July 26 Movement led by Fidel Castro. Also available in a Spanish edition by Editora Política. $23.95

ORDER AT PATHFINDERPRESS.COM

The Second Declaration of Havana

With the First Declaration of Havana

Two manifestos of the Cuban people to the oppressed and exploited throughout the Americas. The first declaration, proclaimed September 1960, calls for "the right of the peasants to the land; the right of the workers to the fruit of their labor; and the right of nations to nationalize the imperialist monopolies." The second declaration, February 1962, asks: "What does the Cuban revolution teach? That revolution is possible." $4.50

Marianas in Combat

Teté Puebla and the Mariana Grajales Women's Platoon in Cuba's Revolutionary War 1956–58

TETÉ PUEBLA

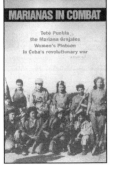

Brigadier General Teté Puebla, the highest-ranking woman in Cuba's Revolutionary Armed Forces, joined the struggle to overthrow the U.S.-backed dictatorship of Fulgencio Batista in 1956, when she was fifteen years old. This is her story—from clandestine action in the cities, to serving as an officer in the victorious Rebel Army's first all-women's unit—the Mariana Grajales Women's Platoon. For nearly fifty years, her life has been intertwined with the fight to transform the social and economic status of women, a course of action inseparable from Cuba's socialist revolution. $14.00

October 1962

The 'Missile' Crisis as Seen from Cuba

TOMÁS DIEZ ACOSTA

In October 1962, during what is widely known as the Cuban Missile Crisis, Washington pushed the world to the edge of nuclear war. Here, for the first time, the full story of that historic moment is told from the perspective of the Cuban people, whose determination to defend the country's sovereignty and their socialist revolution blocked U.S. plans for a military assault and saved humanity from the consequences of a nuclear holocaust. $24.00

Playa Girón / Bay of Pigs

Washington's First Military Defeat in the Americas

FIDEL CASTRO AND JOSÉ RAMÓN FERNÁNDEZ

In less than 72 hours of combat in April 1961, Cuba's revolutionary armed forces defeated an invasion by 1,500 mercenaries organized by Washington. In the process, the Cuban people set an example for workers, farmers, and youth throughout the world that with political consciousness, class solidarity, unflinching courage, and revolutionary leadership, it is possible to stand up to enormous might and seemingly insurmountable odds—and win. In English and Spanish, $20.00

Cuba and the Coming American Revolution

JACK BARNES

There will be a victorious revolution in the United States before there will be a victorious counterrevolution in Cuba. That political fact is at the center of this book. It is about the class struggle in the United States, where the revolutionary capacities of workers and farmers are today as utterly discounted by the ruling powers as were those of the Cuban toilers. And just as wrongly. It is about the example set by the people of Cuba that revolution is not only necessary—it can be made. In English, Spanish, and French, $13.00

Fertile Ground: Che Guevara and Bolivia

A FIRSTHAND ACCOUNT BY RODOLFO SALDAÑA

Told by one of the Bolivians who joined ranks with Ernesto Che Guevara to forge a revolutionary movement of workers, peasants, and young people to overturn the military dictatorship in Bolivia and open the road to socialist revolution in South America. Saldaña talks about the unresolved battles of the tin miners, peasants, and indigenous peoples of his country that created "fertile ground" for Guevara's revolutionary course and mark out the future of Bolivia and the Americas. $9.95

New International

A MAGAZINE OF MARXIST POLITICS AND THEORY

U.S. imperialism has lost the Cold War. That's what the Socialist Workers Party concluded at the opening of the 1990s, in the wake of the collapse of regimes and parties across Eastern Europe and in the USSR that claimed to be communist. Contrary to imperialism's hopes, the working class in those countries had not been crushed. It remains an intractable obstacle to reimposing and stabilizing capitalist relations, one that will have to be confronted by the exploiters in class battles—in a hot war.

Three issues of the Marxist magazine *New International* analyze the propertied rulers' failed expectations and chart a course for revolutionaries in response to rising worker and farmer resistance to the economic and social instability, spreading wars, and rightist currents bred by the world market system. They explain why the historic odds in favor of the working class have increased, not diminished, at the opening of the 21st century.

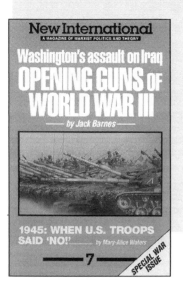

U.S. Imperialism Has Lost the Cold War

JACK BARNES

"It is only from fighters, from revolutionists of action, that communists will be forged in the course of struggle. And it is only from within the working class that the mass political vanguard of these fighters can come. The lesson from over 150 years of political struggle by the modern workers movement is that, more and more, to become and remain a revolutionist means becoming a communist."
In *New International* no. 11. **$14.00**

Imperialism's March toward Fascism and War

JACK BARNES

"There will be new Hitlers, new Mussolinis. That is inevitable. What is not inevitable is that they will triumph. The working-class vanguard will organize our class to fight back against the devastating toll we are made to pay for the capitalist crisis. The future of humanity will be decided in the contest between these contending class forces."
In *New International* no. 10. **$14.00**

Opening Guns of World War III

JACK BARNES

"Washington's Gulf war and its outcome did not open up a new world order of stability and UN-overseen harmony. Instead, it was the first war since the close of World War II that grew primarily out of the intensified competition and accelerating instability of the crises-ridden old imperialist world order." In *New International* no. 7. **$12.00**

ALSO AVAILABLE IN *New International's* SISTER PUBLICATIONS
IN SPANISH, FRENCH, AND SWEDISH

Che Guevara, Cuba, and the Road to Socialism

ARTICLES BY ERNESTO CHE GUEVARA, CARLOS RAFAEL RODRÍGUEZ, CARLOS TABLADA, MARY-ALICE WATERS, STEVE CLARK, JACK BARNES

Exchanges from the early 1960s and today on the political perspectives defended by Guevara as he helped lead working people to advance the transformation of economic and social relations in Cuba. In *New International* no. 8. **$10.00**

The Second Assassination of Maurice Bishop

STEVE CLARK

The lead article in *New International* no. 6 reviews the accomplishments of the 1979-83 revolution in the Caribbean island of Grenada. Explains the roots of the 1983 coup that led to the murder of revolutionary leader Maurice Bishop, and to the destruction of the workers and farmers government by a Stalinist political faction within the governing New Jewel Movement. **$15.00**

The Rise and Fall of the Nicaraguan Revolution

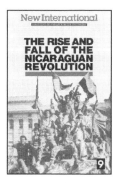

Based on ten years of socialist journalism from inside Nicaragua, this special issue of *New International* recounts the achievements and worldwide impact of the 1979 Nicaraguan revolution. It traces the political retreat of the Sandinista National Liberation Front leadership that led to the downfall of the workers and farmers government in the closing years of the 1980s. Documents of the Socialist Workers Party by Jack Barnes, Steve Clark, and Larry Seigle. In *New International* no. 9. **$14.00**

Distributed by Pathfinder